Edgar
the Se   of the

Golden Flower

Edgar Cayce and the Secret of the Golden Flower

The Ancient Chinese Way to Enlightenment

Taoism

John Van Auken

Director at the Edgar Cayce Foundation

author of
Edgar Cayce and the Kabbalah

A.R.E. Press • Virginia Beach • Virginia

Copyright © 2019
by John Van Auken

1st Printing, January 2020

Printed in the U.S.A.

All rights reserved. No part of this book may be reproduced or transmitted in any form or by any means, electronic or mechanical, including photocopying, recording, or by any information storage and retrieval system, without permission in writing from the publisher.

A.R.E. Press
215 67th Street
Virginia Beach, VA 23451-2061

ISBN-13: 978-0-87604-981-5

Edgar Cayce Readings © 1971, 1993-2007
by the Edgar Cayce Foundation.
All rights reserved.

Cover design by Christine Fulcher

CONTENTS

Book One
Teachings of the Golden Flower of the Great One
[Tai–i Chin–hua tsung–chih)

Book Two
The Book of Consciousness and Life
[Hui Ming Ching)

Illustrations

Teachings of the Old Master . . .

A Brief History and the Key Concepts of Taoism

The word *Tao* may be translated into English as "Way," and is pronounced "dow" (rhymes with *how*), sometimes spelled *Dao*. It is considered to be a Way to physical, mental, and spiritual health.

Taoism has gone through many changes over the past 2,600+ years. Some writers and teachers consider it to be a religion, some believe it is a philosophy, while others teach that it is *a way of life* in harmony with the natural order and flow of life. It did become the official religion of the Tang Dynasty (618–907 CE or AD[1]), which is considered to be the highest cultural period in ancient China, a truly golden age of art, social order, music, and philosophy. Interestingly, given modern feelings about male–dominated leadership, the Tang Dynasty included a female emperor whose name was Wu Zetian.

In the early years of this Dynasty, Confucian scholars ruled the bureaucracy, and examinations were used to test candidates' literary skills and knowledge. A legal code was instituted. The "Silk Road" trade was flourishing, bringing many foreign emissaries to Emperor Taizong and his wonderful country. During this time Buddhism was promoted. The spread of Buddhism was aided with the invention of woodblock printing techniques. Buddhist texts and charms were printed and disseminated. Amazingly, Nestorian *Christianity* was also promoted! In 635 CE, a Nestorian named Alopun traveled to China, and Emperor Taizong approved of the preaching of his religion all over the empire, even ordering the construction of a church in Xian (then ancient Chang'an). Many people became Nestorian Christians. Nestorian Christianity is akin to the Eastern Orthodox Church (from Egypt's Copts up through Greece, Eastern Europe, and into Russia), and these devotees considered Jesus to be a human and Christ to be of God, thus God worked *through* the man–there being two natures, one human and one divine. The preachers of the Eastern Church moved through Asia, while the Western Church moved through *Western* Europe, Britain, and the isles, and on into the Americas.

Today, Taoist precepts and practices have become popular throughout the world and are found in the practice of Tai Chi Chuan (pronounced *tie-chee chew-on*, often called simply, Tai Chi, *tie-chee*), Qigong (pronounced *chee-gong*), and various martial arts, such as Kung Fu and the cultural arts, such as Wushu.

Taoism can be divided into two branches: one seeks a way to physical and social health and well-being, and the other branch seeks a way to eternal reality and immortality. They work *together*, because a healthy physical self makes an excellent temple for an enlightened mind and immortal soul. One sect of Taoism was devoted to conforming to the law of cause and effect, or karma, while transcending the bonds of illusion and confusion. Much of this transcendence is realized through deep reflection and meditation, breathing exercises, and reversing the outflow of energy from the body and the mind. This is what *The Secret of the Golden Flower* is all about.

Master Lao Tzu 老子

The origins of Taoism are generally attributed to a philosopher named Lao Tzu, also known as *Laozi*, and with spelling variations of *Lao Tse, Lao Zi,* and *Lü Tsu.* He is considered to be the author of the classic book, *Tao Te Ching* (this title may be translated into English as, *The Way and Its Virtue* or *The Way and the Power*). Most researchers believe the *Tao Te Ching* was written around 600 BCE (BC²). In *Tao Te Ching* we find the fundamental concepts of Taoism, which we will also find in *The Secret of the Golden Flower,* a book of more modern times.

Who is the true founder of Taoism? The answer is clouded in ancient history, and adding to the challenge is that many teachers carried the *same* name. Here is what we know from two sources: The first, and the oldest source, is the ancient Chinese historian Ssu–ma Ch'ien (145–90 BCE) (pronounced *see-ma chee-en,* where *Ssu-ma* is the family name, *Ch'ien* is his personal name), and his extraordinary work titled *Records of the Grand Historian* (also known by its Chinese name, *Shiji,* approximately pronounced *shoo-tee*). I will use his romanized name, Sima Qian (the "Q" is still pronounced *chee*). The second and more modern source is Youlan Feng's Volume 1 of *A History of Chinese Philosophy,* translated by Derk Bodde, and first published in the 1930s. Feng's book covers the ages from "the *most ancient* origins of *oral* teaching traditions" to about 100 BCE.

According to these two sources, there may have been *three* teachers who contributed to the beginning of Taoism, each carrying the *title* of Lao Tzu! You see, "lao tzu" may be translated into English as *old master, old teacher,* and *old philosopher.* Lao means *old,* and tzu is a term of respect for great teachers/thinkers. Thus, it is not so much a personal name as a descriptive title: 老子. This title could apply to any one of the great teachers in Chinese antiquity. That said, some *specific* person or persons developed and taught the *Tao Te Ching* and established the founding principles that have guided the growth of Taoism.

Sima Qian's search through ancient Chinese history actually found three old masters, any of whom could have been the founder of Taoism. According to Sima Qian, the first "Lao Tzu" was a man named Li Erh (pronounced *Lee er*) from the village of Ch'üjen (pronounced *ch'ing-t'ung*) in the southern Chinese state of Ch'u (pronounced *Ch-oo*). Li Erh served as historian in charge of the official records in the Chinese imperial capital of Luoyang (pronounced *lu-ow-yahng*)—the region where Chinese civilization originated. Luoyang was the ancient capital of China during many of the early dynasties. Li Erh was a contemporary of the well-known philosopher Confucius (551–479 BCE), and Li Erh is reported to have actually *interviewed* Confucius seeking information on the Zhou (pronounced *Joe*). The Zhou ritual is a component of Confucianism dealing with organizational theory (i.e., how to structure and manage bureaucracy). Confucianism is a social and ethical philosophy, with much focus on the ideal way to live and govern.

We know that Li Erh was an *actual* historical entity because we have a great quantity of documentation covering his life and lineage. Some of these documents are like looking at the many "begats" in the Bible. They trace his ancestors and progeny through several generations.

However, the more contemporary historian Youlan Feng writes: "While Ssu-ma Ch'ien [Sima Qian] was aware that Li Erh had been the originator of these documents, he was led astray by the popular talk of his time about *Lao Tan* as their author, and so wrongly assumed Lao Tan and Li Erh to be one person." Youlan considers Lao Tan to be a *mythical* characterization of the *unknown* Father of Taoism. Youlan concedes that Li Erh was an *actual* historical figure who played a role in the origins of Taoism, but was *not* the founder. Considering that Li Erh was a contemporary of Confucius, he had a key relationship that would have encouraged the development of a philosophy. By the way, Confucius was called Con Tzu, meaning *Great Teacher*—adding to our understanding that the word Tzu's meaning is: *teacher, philosopher, master.*

Sima Qian identified a second candidate as the possible founder of Taoism; his name was Lao Lai Tzu. He was the same age as Confucius and wrote a fifteen-chapter book explaining the teachings of a Taoist school. Unfortunately, that book has not survived the passage of the ages and little is known about its contents. There are numerous stories about the debates that supposedly took place between these two great philosophers, in which Lao Lai Tzu was *always* the winner. Today, many believe that these stories are anti-Confucian publicity circulated by members of the Taoist school, perhaps as early as the fourth century BCE.

The third person that Sima Qian considered to be a candidate for the originator of Taoism was a man named *Tan*. It is said that he lived 129 years *after* the death of Confucius (that death would have been roughly 350 BCE). Tan is indeed a historical person. He was one of a long line of historians of Chou (another word for Zhou, pronounced *Joe*). According to Sima Qian, Tan had been serving in the Chou capital for a long time, but he became unhappy with the dishonest political situation and decided to go into retirement. As he was passing through the Hanku Pass west of Luoyang, the gate-keeper stopped him and asked him to write down his teachings. Tan (called *Lao Tzu*) then composed a book of 5,000 sayings in two sections that described the theory of the Tao, and this became the famous *Tao Te Ching*. Some scholars believe that Tan actually wrote down only the *best* of numerous proverbs that had been verbally passed down for centuries, codifying the best of oral tradition into one written text. These scholars studied the style and grammar of the text and found it to reflect the period from 400 to 301 BCE, thus making this third Lao Tzu the likely author of the text. But others before him may well have contributed *orally* to the proverbs and teachings of Taoism. Lao Tzu (Tan) *codified* them in a text. Remember, most scholars date the origin of the concepts and teachings of Taoism back to roughly 600 BCE, long before Tan's writing in the 300s BCE. As with many ancient teachings around the planet, they were mentally perceived, orally taught and memorized, and then passed on through generations.

Tao Te Ching

Since the *Tao Te Ching* is considered to be the foundation upon which Taoism is based, let's briefly look at it. The *Tao Te Ching* (pronounced *dao de ching*) is a book of philosophical sayings in rhyme (they rhyme in Chinese, not in English translations) with stanzas and chapters. Translation is critical to conveying the original meaning, style, and tone, and there are many translations; some are poorly done while others appear to better capture the original poetic style. Throughout this book I will be using a translation by a modern Taoist, Stan Rosenthal, first published in 1984. He is a British scholar and has been acclaimed as having made a faithful and eloquent translation. Remember, the process of reincarnation of souls may return an ancient Chinese philosopher's soul into the new body of a modern British writer—who *innately* has a feel for the original style.

Here is the opening to the *Tao Te Ching* as translated by Rosenthal:

Even the finest teaching is not the Tao itself.
  Even the finest name is insufficient to define it.
  Without words, the Tao can be experienced,
  And without a name, it can be known.
To conduct one's life according to the Tao,
  is to conduct one's life without regrets;
  to realize that potential within oneself
  which is of benefit to all.
Though words or names are not required

to live one's life this way, to describe it,
    words and names are used,
    that we might better clarify the way of which we speak,
    without confusing it with other ways in which
    an individual might choose to live.
Through knowledge, intellectual thought and words,
    the manifestations of the Tao are known,
    but without such intellectual intent
    we might experience the Tao itself.
Both knowledge and experience are real,
    but reality has many forms,
    which seem to cause complexity.
By using the means appropriate,
    we extend ourselves beyond the barriers of such complexity,
    and so experience the Tao.

The most important teachings in the *Tao Te Ching* are found in most all of the great teachings of ancient China, including in *The Secret of the Golden Flower* that we are going to study. Let's look at some examples.

In chapter 16 of the *Tao Te Ching*, titled "Returning to the Root," we find this:

It is only by means of being
    that non-being may be found.

In *being*, or as the Western world taught, "Know Thyself," we may find a way to the serenity, stillness, and inner peace of *non-being*. As in Psalm 46:11, "Be still and know that I am God." Of course, Taoism has no supreme being or personified deity, but the stillness is the *essence* of that which we call "God," or the precondition of *animated life*. Animated life was expressed from infinite silence and stillness. In chapter 21, titled, "Finding the Essence of Tao," we have this:

The essence of Tao is dark and mysterious,
    having, itself, no image or form.
    Yet through its non-being,
    are found image and form.

The essence of Tao is deep and unfathomable,
yet it may be known by not trying to know.

In the origins of Western religion, imagery was used to convey qualities beyond image. For example, elements of ancient Egyptian theology, which Moses bridged to Judaism and Kabbalah, have many symbolic images of various godly influences, often depicting the powers and activities of various animals. For example, jackal-headed Anubis could lead one through the darkness of the underworld to the heavens because, like jackals, he could detect the *scent of the trail* taken from heaven and thereby lead the way back to heaven. The falcon-headed Horus was victorious over his evil uncle Set (depicted as an earthy anteater-like creature) because Horus could see from a higher viewpoint and broader perspective, like a falcon high on the currents of the wind. In early Egyptian temples a *secret* understanding was known about the God/Creator. For example, unlike some of the more standard Egyptian temples, those dedicated to the Sun-god remained open to the sunlight and did *not* feature a statue of the god, because Ra (pronounced *Ray*) was represented *by the sunlight itself*. Adding to this secret teaching was an aspect of god named Amon Ra, who was the *"unseen god."* Moses would have been trained in these secret concepts and would have carried them out of Egypt to the Promised Land.

Once in the desert searching for and being led by God, Moses learned that God was not to be given any form, no image, and no actual name—God gives the name to Moses as, "I am that I am." When Moses's brother Aaron attempted to depict God in the form of a golden calf, it was an abomination to the truth, and was destroyed. Also, when it came to a name, we find in Genesis the word for God is *Elohim* (מיהלא), meaning "deities."[3] Yes, it is plural. It is the plural form of the singular noun *elo'ah* (הולא).[4] Of course, it is clearly understood that Judaism is *monotheistic*, having only one, infinite Divinity, so the plural was likely an attempt by the original authors to maintain a sense that God includes *everything*, and that God was *not separate* from anything. Despite these early concepts, the West took on a "supreme being" approach to God, while Taoism held to a non-being nature of the ultimate essence or spirit from which all emanated and to which all must maintain a connection—since it is the source and sustainer of life. But the point here is that even in the origins of Western theology, no form or image or even name was to be attached to the Divinity. And if we consider the opening lines in the Gospel of John, we find a hint of this in Christianity as well:

"In the beginning was the Word [in Greek this word is actually *Logos*], and the Logos was with God, and the Logos was God. This One [there is no masculine pronoun used here in the original Greek, it is simply, "this One"] was with God in the beginning. Through this One all things were made; without this One nothing was made that has been made. In this One was life, and that life was the light of all humankind. The light shines in the darkness, and the darkness has not overcome it."[5]

Logos (Greek, λόγος) is defined in various ways, such as, the principle of divine reason and creative order, or, the divine reason *implicit* in the cosmos, ordering it and giving it form and meaning. Notice how this takes us beyond a personified deity. Of course, in Christianity the Logos as the Spirit of God descended upon the man Jesus of Nazareth in the image of a dove[6] and *imbued* him with its wisdom and healing powers.

Cayce contributes to this concept of a vast, *impersonal* Creative Force and Universal Consciousness, but he also keeps the *personal* nature of our connection with the Divine. Consider these teachings in the Cayce files:

"This is that portion of the lesson as is to be grounded into the inmost Self until all come to know that not only God is God—there is the One God, the All-Loving God, the Personal God—but the God manifesting through the *individual itself*, for the self is a portion of that Oneness that may make itself at One with the Whole."[7]

Here he responds to a question: "Q: If God is impersonal force or energy . . . [interrupting] A: He *is* impersonal; but as has just been given, so *very* personal! It is not that you deal only with *impersonal*—it is *within and without!* It is *in* and *without*, and only as God *quickens* the spirit within, by the use, by the application of the God-force within to mete it out to others."[8] "Mete" is a biblical term meaning "measure out." Here Cayce is teaching that as we engage with others in our relationships, the flow of the life-giving Divine comes through in a personalized manner from the infinite, impersonal source of life and light.

Here's one more Cayce teaching that reveals his broader perspective on the nature of God, using a Kabbalistic view of the Great I AM and the little I am.

"Take that answer into your secret chambers of your heart and, with your communion with your God, your god-self, that I AM that you must proclaim as the impelling influence in the hearts and souls of men, answer *there!*"[9]

In the context of the essence or spirit as the source and sustainer of life, Taoism sought to reconnect firmly to this source, and in fact, live incarnate while mindfully and physically in oneness with this source. This is their way toward longevity and immortality, and is a constant theme in Taoist teachings and practices.

In chapter 40 of the *Tao Te Ching*, titled, "Being and Not Being," we find this:

> The motion of nature
>   is cyclic and returning.
> Its way is to yield,
>   for to yield is to become.
> All things are born of being;
>   being is born of non-being.

The fundamental teaching is that we were initially conceived in a non-being oneness with the infinite, eternal *essence*, and that portion of us is still in us, deep inside our being. However, the journey through beingness is important, purposeful, and is a natural portion of life's journey. It is motion, it is cyclical (birth, life, death, rebirth), and these cycles are meant to build understanding and wisdom, and lead us to become our true selves—knowing ourselves to be our selves yet one with the Whole.

In chapter 51, titled, "The Nourishment of the Tao," we find this:

> All living things are formed by being,
>   and shaped by their environment,
>   growing if nourished well by virtue;
>   the being from non-being.

Virtue nourishes us. Our creative nature seeks to express life and shape life as it fits circumstances, and it is virtue that nourishes our creations, our being, and our surroundings.

The Secret of the Golden Flower, as with most all Taoist teachings, is a training into how being can rebirth or reawaken nonbeing in the womb of our consciousness, and we are once again whole—that is, non-being essence and expressed being are one.

A Brief History of the Secret of the Golden Flower

Important Background

As is true with most of the world's ancient teachings, they were only *orally* conveyed for many, many generations, then eventually written down. Legend traces the origin of the Golden Flower *concepts* (not text) to the 700s CE (AD), but the first known *printed* text was a wood-block printing in the 1700s. As you can see, it is a relatively modern document. However, its origins go back many centuries.

The title is actually *Tai-i Chin-hua tsung-chih*, literally translated as *Teachings of the Golden Flower of the Great One*. The "Great One" in this case is that above which there is nothing and out of which *all* emanated. Kabbalah refers to this original One as the "Infinite Eternal" (Hebrew: אֵין סוֹף, *Ein Sof*), which we may consider to be "God," but again not as a supreme *being* but an infinite, eternal *essence*. However, the use of the term "One" implies a central, singular source, a central *monad*—defined by the philosophy of Leibniz as an *indivisible* and hence ultimately simple *One*.[10] In both the Golden Flower teaching and the Kabbalah, God is not a personality or being, but is personified *through* the beings that emanated out of this One, infinite, eternal source and sustainer of life—life that is both seen and unseen. Our scientists have discovered that most of the universe is *unseen*. They know this because *something* much bigger than the material universe is affecting matter. They have determined that our *seen* universe is only 4% of the whole universe! Fortunately, our journey with the *Golden Flower* is going to take us into the other 96%—the potent unseen behind it all.

As to who actually wrote *The Secret of the Golden Flower*, it is difficult to be certain of this; and remember, those generations who taught it *orally* are very different from who actually *wrote* it and then printed it. The work is attributed to Lü Yen (700s CE), also known as Lü Tung-pin, and simply as Lü of the Cavern.[11] Baynes tells us that Lü attributes his wisdom to a sage known as Kuan Yin-hsi, the "Master of the Pass." Legend holds that Kuan Yin-hsi was the gatekeeper at the Hanku Pass who asked Tan, one of Ssu-ma Ch'ien's possible Lao Tzu authors of the *Tao Te Ching*, to write down his teachings. If so, this would have dated Kuan Yin-hsi to the 300s BCE. If Lü Yen studied the teachings of Kuan Yin-hsi, he was likely studying Lao Tzu's *Tao Te Ching*. And we have seen how the teachings about being and non-being originated in the *Tao Te Ching*.

If you search on the internet you will find a Wikipedia site claiming that the author of the *Golden Flower* was Lü Dongbin (somewhere between 796 and 1016 CE). Actually, *Dongbin* is a romanization of the more proper *Tung-pin*. According to this Wikipedia report, he was "a Tang Dynasty Chinese scholar and poet who has been elevated to the status of an immortal in the Chinese cultural sphere, worshiped especially by the Taoists. Lü is one of the most widely known of the group of deities known as the Eight Immortals. He is also a historical figure who was mentioned in the official history book *History of Song*." His name is Lü Yán, with Yán being the given name. *Tung-pin* is an honorary title. Lü is widely considered to be one of the earliest masters of the tradition of *neidan*. Neidan is a collection of esoteric doctrines and practices that Taoist initiates used, and some continue to use, to prolong life and create an immortal spiritual body that will survive death of the physical body.

The *Golden Flower's* teachings also seek this end: conceiving, gestating, and birthing the spiritual body so as to live on beyond physical death.

The Challenge with Translation

There are two popular and competing English translations of *The Secret of the Golden Flower*. One was by Englishman Cary F. Baynes, who translated Richard Wilhelm's *German* translation, with many notes about the challenges of translation and the peculiarities of Wilhelm's method. Baynes's editions were published in 1931 and a revised edition in 1962. Richard Wilhelm was a sinologist who had purchased an old text while being trained in China by a Taoist teacher named Lau Nai Suan. Wilhelm's original German translation contained a commentary by Swiss depth-psychologist Dr. Carl Jung. The other competing English translation was done by Thomas Cleary in 1991.

A lesser known translation, but often seen on the internet, is an abbreviated translation by Walter Picca, published in 1964. Picca does not cover the whole text and has his own way of interpreting the original meaning, which I will mention occasionally as we study.

The more well-known translation by Cleary claims that Wilhelm's German translation was "a garbled translation of a truncated version of a corrupted recension of the original work."[12] Cleary also wrote, "Because the still-current Wilhelm/Jung/Baynes edition of this manual contains dangerous and misleading contaminations, a primary consideration of the translation was to make the contents of *The Secret of the Golden Flower* explicitly accessible to both lay and specialist audiences. This is partly a matter of translation and partly a matter of presentation."[13]

Another detail is that only the Wilhelm/Jung/Baynes edition includes a second Taoist manuscript titled, *Hui Ming Ching*, meaning: *The*

Book of Life and Consciousness. It is significant to our full understanding and practice. It was written by the Ch'an Buddhist monk Liu Huayang in 1794. It is *not* included in the Cleary or Picca translations. It was first translated in German by Wilhelm and published in 1926 under the title of *Liu Hua Yang, Hui Ming King. Das Buch von Bewusstsein und Leben*. Later this German translation was translated into French, and printed in 1934 with title of *Lieou Hua Yang. Le Livre de la Conscience et de la Vie*. A Russian translation was made by V.V. Maliavin. There is also a translation by Eva Wong, titled *Cultivating the Energy of Life*.

In order to compare the translation by Wilhelm and Baynes against a scholastic translation, I have found the Master of Arts thesis by James Michael Nicholson, published in 2000 and titled: *The Huiming Jing: A Translation and Discussion*. It was in the Open Collection of the library of the University of British Columbia.[14] As Baynes did, Nicholson acknowledges how the unique use of language and symbolism in the manuscript "is particularly complex and does not lend itself to easy interpretation or understanding." Throughout his thesis he footnotes details about various Taoist terms used by Liu Huayang and others, adding to our greater understanding of the teacher's intention. Nicholson points out that Wilhelm only translated the opening to each section of this classic manuscript, not the subsequent material. Nicholson also points out how Wilhelm's prejudice toward Jungian psychology "does not provide an accurate representation of what is communicated in the original Chinese. This is primarily due to the fact that Wilhelm presents the teachings in a way that makes them appear to be a form of proto–Jungian psychology, which ignores the basic conceptions found not only in inner alchemy, but in the Taoist and Chinese traditions in general regarding the make–up of human beings."[15] Nicholson also felt that although Eva Wong's text is readable and "provides a reasonable introduction to the world of inner alchemical training that is more accurate than that provided by Wilhelm," she leaves out whole sections of the original text rendering it "inadequate for those with an academic interest in precision."

Where it is helpful, I'll share Nicholson's translation and comments.

Furthermore, because there is a third book mentioned in the *Golden Flower*, which I found to be helpful, I have included a few key teachings from the Taoist text titled: *The Jade Emperor's Mind Seal Classic*—translated by Stuart Alve Olson, and published in English in 1992 by Dragon Door Publications. Actually, the title is more correctly titled *Mind Seal* or *Book of the Seal of the Heart*, where the *Heart* is a heavenly *consciousness*, or a state of mind. Olson shared a helpful insight when he wrote: "The real difficulty in doing this [translation] however is that the verses of the text are in the framework of mystical experience. The language of the mystics is very difficult to adapt into everyday language, for the very nature of the mystical experience is beyond normal mundane experiences and language."[16]

I must reveal to you, my reader, that I grew in understanding, energy, and enlightenment using the Wilhelm/Jung/Baynes edition. I began studying and practicing the *Golden Flower* teachings in my early twenties, and practiced consistently. I had read and reread the Wilhelm/Jung/Baynes edition over and over and practiced the meditation techniques and psychological concepts faithfully for many years—*with profound results!* I took training classes with elders using that edition. It wasn't until my mid-forties that I read Cleary's translation. Initially, I was turned off by Cleary's edition. It felt uninspired and cold, spiritless. Its translation might be more accurate but it felt lifeless, missing the spirit of the words and concepts. Nevertheless, gradually I came to appreciate Cleary's version in certain parts of the ancient text. However, being true to my experiences and success with the Wilhelm/Jung/Baynes edition, and discontented with the whole of Cleary's text, I still prefer the spiritual, celestial focus in the Wilhelm/Jung/Baynes edition. Therefore, that version is the translation that I will use in this book. Nevertheless, I will reveal how Cleary translated certain lines from the ancient text, especially when it adds to or improves our understanding.

Our translation challenges begin with the opening line of the classic text. Thomas Cleary translated the opening passage as, "Naturalness is called the Way"; Walter Picca translated it as, "That which exist through itself is called Meaning (Tao)." The Wilhelm/Baynes translated this opening as: "That which exist through itself is called the Way (Tao)." I preferred the use of the word "Way" over the others. This may have something to with *my prejudice* toward the term "the Way," which was the name attached to Jesus's movement by the early Jews who practiced his concepts and methods: της οδου—Greek for "the Way."

Being a mystical Christian *and* a believer in a *universal* truth woven into all belief systems, I look for similarities in most all cultures, religions, and geographic locations. I find them everywhere. However, most writers attribute this name—"the Way"—to a well-known statement by Jesus: "I am the way, the truth, and the life. No one comes to the Father except through Me."[17] Many Christians use this statement to claim that their faith is the only true faith, but Edgar Cayce turned this statement into a more *universal* meaning, teaching that Jesus was the man, Christ was the spirit *in* the man: *"Christ* is not a man! *Jesus* was the man; Christ the messenger; Christ in all ages, Jesus in one."[18] The name "Christ" is a transliteration of the Greek word "christos," meaning "anointed one," exactly the meaning of the Hebrew word "mashiach," which is transliterated as "messiah." From Cayce's universal attunement, the messianic presence is a *consciousness* of the Source of all life, the Creative Forces, the Universal Consciousness, or God. Jesus taught that our relationship to God is as God's children or *emanations* from the Source of all Life. The ancient Egyptians called us "godlings" of the great God—rays of the great RA (pronounced *ray*).[19] As such, Jesus used the name *Father.* When he made this famous statement ("No one comes to the Father except through me.") he was referring to the *consciousness* that he had of the infinite, eternal, heavenly Father/Mother. He, the man, was *connected* to this consciousness, and he told us that all he taught and did was shown to him by the Father.[20] This connection came to him by the God-consciousness that he received when the Holy Spirit descended upon him when John baptized him.[21] We could clarify his statement as: "The *consciousness* of the Source of Life, our Father/Mother, is the way, the truth, and the life." This is not to diminish Jesus in any way, but rather to expand his meaning as *inclusive* of any souls anywhere whose minds have expanded to the greater awareness of the *essence* or *spirit* that is the source of life. Jesus actually implied this when he warned us, speaking as the Good Shepherd: "Other sheep I have, which are *not of this fold;* them also I must bring, and they shall hear my voice; and there shall be one fold, and one shepherd."[22] The sheep that are not of this fold ("this fold" being the "chosen people" of the Jews listening to him) may include many more than those who know Christianity. It may be those who connect with the God-consciousness as Jesus did. The "one shepherd" is likely the "Great One" or "Infinite Oneness" of Taoism and Kabbalah.

As I already shared, Nestorian Christianity was in China from the 7th through the 10th centuries, and later during the Mongol Yuan Dynasty in the 13th and 14th centuries. Locally, the religion was known as Jingjiao/Ching-chiao (景教), which literally means the "Luminous Religion." Again, let me make it clear that Nestorian Christianity is akin to the Eastern European Church or Orthodox Church, and these believers considered Jesus to be a human and Christ to be of Divine Spirit that worked *through* the man—there being two natures, one human and one divine. This concept will help us as we study the *Golden Flower* teachings and practice the meditations.

A Little About Edgar Cayce

I was 16 years old when I first read an Edgar Cayce book on life, holistic health, and personal spirituality. Now, more than 60 years later, to me he is still one of the best sources of spiritual wisdom—that is, second to one's own *inner* wisdom—which is the *best* source, and this inner source brings the greater soul growth. With that said, Cayce's information is an excellent guideline along the way to enlightenment.

Let me briefly explain why he is a part of this book.

The first reason is that he taught the value of and encouraged the practice of *deep* meditation. His concepts concerning deep meditation and his methods for achieving the deeper levels nicely complement those in *The Secret of the Golden Flower.*

Second, over the many incarnations of his soul, Cayce often sought and even possessed enlightenment, and he was moved to share that enlightenment with any who wanted to hear it. In this recent incarnation he possessed an innate ability to put himself into a trance-like state and tune his mind to what he called the *Universal Consciousness*. This was the source and container of all life. He would channel what came to him as well as answer questions asked of him. In this state he explained and demonstrated that every soul was connected to this collective consciousness, and he could access them wherever they were—even if they were *not* incarnate! And though he was a devoted Christian, the wisdom that came through him was universal, and often contained elements of ancient philosophy and theologies, such as Hinduism, ancient Egyptian mysticism, and even Taoism—our subject matter here.

All I ask of you is to consider his insights as I share them along with the Taoist master's. If they are helpful, great. If they don't add anything to your soul growth, leave them. Please don't let them get in the way of your soul search. Even Cayce stated that one's journey and growth are individual, and must find a place within each individual.[25]

Cayce has been called the "Father of Holistic Medicine" by the *Journal of the American Medical Association* (JAMA 1979:241(11):1156), because in the 1920s, '30s, and '40s he was teaching that health must take into consideration the *whole* person: body, mind, *and* soul. Attempting to fix just one part would not result in true, lasting health. All of his discourses are called "readings" because it appeared that he was *reading* the Book of Life or the Akashic Record of individual souls or soul groups that inquired of him. He is also the most documented channel that I know of, and most researchers agree. All of his "readings" are cataloged and given numbers, mostly to maintain the privacy of the those inquiring, but also for fast access. In this book I will not burden you with these reference numbers as we read, but will list them in the Endnotes. Also, the language of his channeled comments is difficult for us to read today, because he spoke in what we may call "King–James–Bible English." To help with this, I have updated his language and syntax and extracted only those words that address our study. He could give some of the most complex and long sentences that I have ever come across, and these sentences would contain multiple topics. If you ever want to see the original text, go to the endnotes, get the reference number, and then you can look up the original and see how I have modified it for our study. Mostly, I have changed "thee" and "thou" and the like to modern terms.

I first read his verbatim teachings and began practicing them in my mid–twenties through my thirties. Fortunately, I had training in the metaphysical meaning of allegorical words. By the time I came across the *Golden Flower* teachings, I understood that "Heavenly Heart between the sun and moon" was actually the place of my deeper mind and its view from behind my two eyes. This fit well with my study of ancient Egyptian wisdom in which the right eye represented the sun and was called the "eye of Ra," while the left represented the moon and was known as the "eye of Horus." I also came to understand that the "square inch *field* in the square foot *house*" represented my mind as a "field" inside my head as a "house." I came to understand that the upper chakras that help us find our way to enlightenment are functioning through the physical combination of the pituitary, hypothalamus, and pineal glands inside our brains. I knew this because Edgar Cayce taught that the endocrine glands of the human body correlated with the chakras found in the ancient *Yoga Sutra*. They play an essential role in raising our vibrations and expanding our consciousness. Since the body is a temporary temple of our soul-mind, these glands may shift their hormonal messages from earthly needs to spiritual needs—creating a more ideal environment for our soul-mind while incarnate.

I also had enough training to know about *essence* versus *substance*, or *energy* versus *matter*, and how these related to our *whole* being. All of us are three-dimensional beings in material bodies—but that is just the *substance*. We are also energy beings or sparks of life incarnating *through* these material bodies. With this in mind, it is clear that the Taoist teacher was directing us to *reverse* the flow of our life force (energy) from only outward expression to "backward flowing"—thereby subduing the material body and outer mind for the purpose of reigniting our *inner* essence and *heavenly* awareness.

During this period of my life I was studying with others my age under the tutelage of two elder teachers at the Edgar Cayce center in Virginia Beach, Virginia. The two teachers were Hugh Lynn Cayce, president of the Association for Research and Enlightenment and author of the book *Venture Inward*; and Herbert Bruce Puryear, Ph.D., who understood the Cayce teachings and could explain them in ways that few others could. These teachers combined mystical Christianity with Jungian psychology, which they felt fit nicely with many of the lessons by the Old Master of the *Golden Flower*, especially since Dr. Carl Jung's commentary was included in Richard Wilhelm's original book.

An Important Note

Remember that there were *many* teachers called Lao Tzu, and there were many variations of this name. Since "lao tzu" literally means something akin to *old master*, there could be, and I am certain there were, many old masters teaching the Tao and the Golden Flower. In the Wilhelm/Jung/Baynes edition the opening line begins with: "Master Lü Tzu said . . . " Lü Tzu is a variation of the name Lao Tzu. However, the "Old Master" of *The Secret of the Golden Flower* is not the original author of the *Tao Te Ching*. With this in mind I have changed the opening line to read: "The Old Master said." Throughout this book I will replace Lü Tzu with the descriptive title, "Old Master."

Also, Baynes's translation uses British English and spelling. In the translation text I have changed that to American English and spelling, but when Baynes is speaking for himself, I leave his British English as he wrote it. Thus, color is *colour*, splendor is *splendour*, and Baynes's *to-day* remains *to-day*. Other such uniquenesses of Baynes's writing have been changed to fit American English, unless he is specifically expressing himself. Also, Englishman Baynes and Swiss psychologist Carl Jung use the quote-marks system found in British English, thus single quote marks come *first*, double quote marks come *within* the single marks. I have left their style as they wrote it when expressing their thoughts.

Any words or phrases in (parentheses) are the *original* comments of either of the two translators—in some cases it is Wilhelm and in some it is Baynes. My comments are in [brackets]. I have also changed the *type font* to help us easily see the changes in who is actually speaking: the Old Master, Wilhelm, Baynes, or I.

A Warning

The concepts in this Taoist text are true and the methods are effective. They will help us awaken our true selves that have been dormant for too long. However, we are presently incarnate in a world of people and places, relationships, companionships, and physical needs and obligations. We have talents and drives that need expression through this incarnation. We have karma that needs resolution. And our presence can make life better for those with whom we share life. The lessons in this *Golden Flower* text will take us far away from this reality; for us to keep our sanity we must deftly straddle the two realities—finite/personal and infinite/impersonal—consciously maintaining a *balance*. This incarnation by our souls was intentional and purposeful; and we have an important role here. At the same time, our souls long for the transcending illumination that reveals our ultimate destiny and eternal nature.

In *The Jade Emperor's Mind Seal Classic* we find that the old masters knew this need for balance, as we see in this teaching: "Keep to non-being, yet hold onto being, and perfection is yours . . . "[24] As we expand our awareness into the infinite from out of our finite lives, we need to be careful and mindful of holding these two realities in balance while actively involved in both!

The key to maintaining balance is love. This love is expressed in the two great commandments: love God and love one another. The teachings and practices in this text will take us to that serene, contented love within the Infinite Eternal Oneness from which we have emanated. But we can get lost there and lose sight of our role in this world with other souls. It helps if we keep in mind that the Infinite Eternal One loves these other souls just as it loves us, and may use us to express its love for them by our presence in their lives—and their presence in our lives.

In my 50-plus years of practicing balance, I have noticed that at various times I was more involved in love with the Infinite, while at others times I was actively involved in love with the many finite relationships with other souls. Eventually, this became less extreme, and was more easily balanced. In fact, each day has both the inner, infinite love connection and the outer, life-contributing love with other souls. It required consciously budgeting time for both, and being mindful of the role of both realities.

One of the main abilities of the Egyptian god Thoth, Hermes in Greek, was that he could live between the realities—this world and at the same time in the realms of the Heavens. This was symbolized in his icon which contained both the Sun and Moon, indicating that he was conscious of the direct source of Light (Sun) but also able to reflect that Light when in the dimmer reality of this world (Moon).

Depth psychologist Carl Jung also sees a warning for Western minds: "We should do well to confess at once that, fundamentally speaking, we do not understand the complete detachment from the world of a text like this, indeed, that we do not want to understand it. Have we, perhaps, an inkling that a mental attitude which can direct the glance inward to this extent can bring about such detachment only because these people have so completely fulfilled the instinctive demands of their natures that little or nothing prevents them from viewing the invisible essence of the world? Can it be, perhaps, that the premise of such vision is liberation from those ambitions and passions which bind us to the visible world, and does not this liberation result from the sensible fulfillment of instinctive demands, rather than from the premature or fear-born repression of them? Is it that our eyes are opened to the spirit only when the laws of earth are obeyed? Anybody who knows the history of Chinese culture, and has also carefully studied the *I Ching* ["Book of Changes"], that book of wisdom which for thousands of years has permeated all Chinese thought, will not pass over these questions lightly. He will know, moreover, that the views set forth in our text are nothing extraordinary from the Chinese point of view, but are actually inescapable, psychological conclusions. In our Christian culture, spirit, and the passion of the spirit, were for a long time the greatest values and the things most worth striving for. Only after the decline of the Middle Ages, that is, in the course of the 19th century, when spirit began to degenerate into intellect, did a reaction set in against the unbearable dominance of intellectualism. This movement, it is true, at first committed the pardonable mistake of confusing intellect with spirit, and blaming the latter for the misdeeds of the former. Intellect does, in fact, harm the soul when it dares to possess itself of the heritage of the spirit. It is in no way fitted to do this, because spirit is something higher than intellect in that it includes not only the latter, but the feelings as well. It is a direction, or principle, of life that strives towards shining, supra-human heights."

Let us try to be mindful when we are too far *from* this reality or too deeply absorbed *in this* reality. Strive for the *balance*, and the ideal will be ours. As Hermes did, try to bridge the two realities. Just as the Taoist master taught: "Keep to non-being, yet hold onto being, and perfection is yours."

The Layout

The original Wilhelm/Jung/Baynes edition contains two sections. The first is titled, "The Secret of the Golden Flower," which is followed by the section titled, "The Book of Consciousness and Life." The first section begins with a short chapter titled, "Heavenly Consciousness of the Heart" and proceeds through eight short chapters followed by a Summary. The second section begins with the chapter title, "Cessation of Outflowing," and proceeds through another eight chapters. As you may already know, eight is the luckiest number in Chinese culture because 八 sounds like 發 (fa), which means "wealth," "fortune," and "prosper" in Chinese. Thus, eight chapters in each section is ideal from a Chinese perspective.

Remember, words in parentheses belong to Wilhelm or Baynes. Any parenthetical statements belonging to the origin text remain in the type font used for the original text. Words in brackets are mine or a source that I will identify. Endnotes provide details, and may be found in the back of this book.

Here follows the original text of both books.

Book One

Teachings of the Golden Flower of the Great One

Translation of the
T'ai-i Chin Hua Tsung Chih

The Way, Essence and Life, the One, the Light,
Action to Non-Action, the Backward Flow,
a Second Body, and the Circulation of the Light

1. Heavenly Consciousness of the Heart

The Old Master said: That which exists through itself is called the Way (Tao).[25] Tao [the Way] has neither name nor shape. It is the one essence, the one primal spirit. Essence and life cannot be seen.

In a footnote Baynes tells us that this is the only time he is going use the English word "essence" to translate the Chinese word *hsing*, from here on he will translate this word as "human nature." I understand why he made this decision, but it will limit our understanding if we don't add more—especially since the term is going to be used differently in the second section that we are going to study, the *Book of Consciousness and Life*. In that section *hsing* is being translated as "consciousness." *Hsing* has a few meanings in Chinese, and it can be combined with other words to provide even more meanings. It truly can be translated as "human nature," but it is not so much a *physical* human but the *essentiality* of *being* human. *Hsing-Ming* is a well-known concept in Taoism where "ming" means the human body and "hsing" means the quality of the entity *inside* that body. We have to be careful with this because these teachings are also going to speak about a *life force* within the human and its body, and Baynes is going to translate that as "life," thus we have: *Consciousness and Life*.

1

For our better understanding we may think of the *life force* as the élan vital of the Western world. We may think of it in two ways, one is the Old Master's term "vital breath." This fits with chapter two of Genesis where we were given life when the Lord God (*Yahweh Elohim*) breathed the "breath of life" into us, and we became "living souls."[26] This breath would be akin to Hinduism's *prana*, "life-giving breath." But we also have the élan in the more material aspects of our physical bodies as the *kundalini* with ch'i (pronounced *ch-ee*, also spelled *qi*) Thus, we have a physical body (*ming*), we have our human essence (*hing*), and we have energy (*ch'i*) in the form of vital breath.

Now back to the Old Master's teaching about essence and life:

> They [essence and life] are contained in the Light of Heaven. The light of Heaven cannot be seen. It is contained in the two eyes. Today I will be your guide and will first reveal to you the secret of the Golden Flower of the great One, and, starting from that, I will explain the rest in detail.
>
> The great One is the term given to that which has nothing above it. The secret of the magic of life consists in using action in order to attain non-action. One must not wish to leap over everything and penetrate directly. The maxim handed down to us is to take in hand the work on the human nature (*hsing*). In doing this it is important not to take any wrong path.

We have just been given one of the most fundamental teachings of Taoism: there are certain actions that will naturally lead us to the necessary serenity of *non-action*, which is required in order for us to experience the illumination and revitalization of the Golden Flower. Also, the teacher instructs us not to attempt to leap directly to the fullness of this practice, but to proceed step-by-step, not leaving out any steps. The journey is as important as the destination.

Edgar Cayce also taught this: "Remember the law. It is the little leaven that leavens the whole lump. Again would it be repeated—it is here a little, there a little, line upon line, precept upon precept."[27] Cayce is referring to one of Jesus's parables: "He told them another parable. 'The kingdom of heaven is like leaven which a woman took and hid in three measures of flour, till it was all leavened.'"[28] Keep in mind that the woman had to knead the leaven into the bread dough, over and over until it was fully and evenly in the dough. We must do the same to fully and evenly knead the light into our whole being.

The Old Master is guiding us to be patient and apply each portion of the training rather than attempt to skip portions and seek the whole experience before we are ready.

> The Golden Flower is the Light. What color is the light? One uses the Golden Flower as a symbol. It is the true energy of the transcendent great One. The phrase, "The lead of the water-region has but one taste," refers to it.
>
> The work on the circulation of the Light depends entirely on the backward-flowing movement, [see p. 4] so that the thoughts (the place of Heavenly Consciousness, the Heavenly Heart) [illustration for Stage 1: "Gathering the Light" p. 14] are gathered together. The Heavenly Heart lies between sun and moon (i.e., between the two eyes).

The Old Master is preparing us to open our minds to meaning *beyond* appearances, meaning expressed in metaphors, symbols, and emblems. Words cannot easily convey *essence*, so we have to learn to *feel*, *imagine*, and *intuit* the deeper truths and messages beyond the physical words and stories. Nothing is literal, everything is a parable, an allegory relating to an infinite, eternal reality beyond physical reality.

How will we know if we are correctly discerning the deeper meaning? We will *feel* the truth or falsehood *intuitively*, because all of us have been conceived with this knowledge implanted in our hearts and minds. This is what the Old Master means by, "the lead of the water-region has but one taste." *We intuitively know that taste.* When we are truly tasting the "water of life," we will *innately* know it. This follows Jesus's teaching that no one ascends to heaven who did not already *descend* from heaven.[29] Our original, deeper self is familiar with our heavenly origin and has not forgotten it. It is inborn and accessible. By the way, Cleary translates this phrase: "The lead in the homeland of water is just one flavor." I think of the "homeland of water" as the heavenly realms of our origin. We are only temporarily incarnating as terrestrial beings, we are eternally celestial beings.

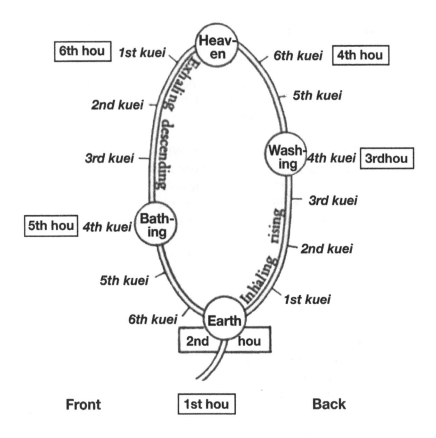

| 6th hou | 1st kuei | Heaven | 6th kuei | 4th hou |

Front   1st hou   **Back**

This diagram by Buddhist monk Liu Huayang in 1794, depicts the circulation of the light breathing pattern. *Hou* means "time," but here it represents the two lower chakras (which live in time, present and ancient). *Kuei* (pronounced *gway* also *gwee*) means *reversal, return,* and *renewal,* but here it's a counted rhythm of *turns*—six up and six down. As one opens the lower region of the body, one inhales breath *upward* through the spinal column (right side of diagram, the "control–path" *tu*). This is both a physical and visualized raising. This is "washing" of earthiness through six levels. We are returning or *backward flowing* the breath. In the upper region associated with heaven, we close and

abide there, uniting with heavenly breath. The left side of the diagram depicts, the "function-path" *jen*, exhaling and "bathing" the six
levels with the united breath (earth and heaven). As the lung-breath
moves, so does the light and life-force (vital breath).

The master's "backward flowing" teaching is also key to our enlightenment. Our spiritual self entered our baby body through the
fontanelle (soft spot at the top of the skull), which is also the crown
chakra. We pushed our essence into the body's nervous system, and
then developed an *outward* projection of consciousness as we grew in
this material reality. Today, we continue to utilize our life energy in an
outward direction most all of the time. If we are to awaken and reconnect
with our original spiritual, soul self and its creative source, we need to
reverse the flow of consciousness inward through reflection and meditation. We also need to reverse the flow of our life energy from outward
projection to inward rejuvenation, revivification, and revitalization.

Back to the original text.

> *The Book of the Yellow Castle* says: "In the square inch field
> of the square foot house, life can be regulated." The square
> foot house is the face. The square inch field in the face: what
> could that be other than the Heavenly Heart? In the middle of
> the square inch dwells the splendor. In the purple hall of the
> city of jade dwells the God of Utmost Emptiness and Life.[30]
> The Confucians call it the center of emptiness; the Buddhists,
> the terrace of life; the Taoists, the ancestral land, or the yel-
> low castle, or the dark pass, or the space of former Heaven.
> The heavenly heart is like the dwelling place, the Light is the
> master.
>
> Therefore, when the Light circulates, the energies of the
> whole body appear before its throne, as, when a holy king
> has established the capital and has laid down the funda-
> mental rules of order, all the states approach with tribute,
> or as, when the master is quiet and calm, men-servants and
> maids obey his orders of their own accord, and each does
> his work.

Here, the master's reference to *The Book of the Yellow Castle* is likely referring to *The Yellow Court Classic*, a Taoist meditation text dated to around 288 CE and written by Lady Wei Huacun, one of the founders of the "Highest Purity Tradition." She was one of many wise Taoist women teachers. There were also Buddhist *nun* sages (*bhikkhunī* or *bhikṣuṇī*), one of whom taught the famous Bodhidharma (400s CE). There were women pharaohs in Egypt, and Muslim women of great wisdom as teachers and poets in the original, classical Sufism in Turkey (then Anatolia).

The Yellow Court Classic is a highly symbolic text in which the "Castle" is the realm of the four Chinese alchemical elements: metal, water, wood, and fire. These are elements of the *earthly* realm, while spirit or pure energy is the element of heavenly realms.

Notice the paradoxical "field" being *within* a "house." This is a poetic way of conveying to us how vast and fertile the realm of our deeper mind is when it is awakened. The color of "the hall of the city of jade" had to be *purplish*, for the chakras (spiritual centers and endocrine glands) reflect the *spectrum* cast when white light enters into the *prism* of our human bodies. That spectrum results in these colors, which may be correlated in order to each chakra: red, orange, yellow, green, blue, indigo, and violet. It is seen in the rainbow. The spiritual centers or chakras correlate to our seven major endocrine glands: gonads, cells of Leydig, adrenals, thymus, thyroid, pineal, and pituitary.

The amazing pineal gland deep inside our brain contains features that are also found in our eyes. Many consider that the "rods" and "cones" in the pineal gland (in the dark recesses of the brain) act as light–transducers that are getting their light from a source way beyond the physical realms. Thus, the pineal has long been considered to be the Third Eye, an eye that sees beyond physical reality.

Physically the pineal creates and secretes melatonin, which is passed on to all portions of our body through our circulatory system. The pineal detects changes in our environment (both internal and external changes), and generates our circadian rhythms accordingly. Serotonin is the precursor to melatonin, and is a hormone linked to good feelings, or "good vibrations." The pineal gland also stores serotonin in large quantities. This is necessary because the 40 million cells in our brains use serotonin to communicate and interact.

Additionally, there is a growing belief that the pineal gland also produces a psychedelic chemical or chemicals that allow us to enter into other dimensions of consciousness. We find a hint of this in the "imaginative forces" described by Edgar Cayce in a discourse on the pineal gland:

"There are definite conditions that arise from within the inner man when an individual enters into true or deep meditation. A physical condition happens, a physical activity takes place! Acting through what? Through that man has chosen to call the imaginative or the impulsive, and the sources of impulse are aroused by the shutting out of thought pertaining to activities or attributes of the carnal forces of man. ... Then, changes naturally take place when there is the arousing of that stimuli within the individual that has within it the seat of the soul's dwelling, within the individual body of the entity or man, and then this partakes of the individuality rather than the personality."[31]

In Cayce's lexicon, the "individuality" is the inner soul or psyche and the "personality" is the outer, incarnate, and temporary portion of our being. And Cayce's "seat of the soul" is in the "lyden" center, the second chakra, often referred to as the navel chakra (named "cells of Leydig" after the doctor who first discovered them). Cayce taught, "The glandular forces then are ever akin to the sources from which, through which, the soul dwells within the body."[32] Interestingly, in an effort to help a woman suffering with health challenges, Cayce revealed that the lyden center and the pineal gland communicate through the cerebrospinal and sympathetic nervous systems, and that these two glands were functioning well in this woman but that she was more "soul sick than physically sick."[33] So often we become more soul sick than physically sick because physicality does not feed our souls with the nourishment it seeks.

In this higher chakra of our body, the pineal, dwells "the god of utmost emptiness and life." Who is this god? We are all godlings of God, as described in Genesis 1:26 and Psalm 82:6. Why emptiness and life? Think of a womb, how quiet and empty it is, and yet it possesses all the potential for life! Such is the condition that we will experience when we enter the former place of our spiritual birth. Here again I am reminded of one of Jesus's famous teachings to Nicodemus: "You must be born again."[34] Unfortunately, Nicodemus's mind was so materially focused that he asked Jesus how he could get back into his mother's womb. Jesus must have wondered how he was going to give this important teaching to such a materialistic man. Jesus then explained to Nicodemus that the physical self has been born, but now he must give birth to his spiritual self. Thus, Nicodemus—and all of us—must conceive our spirit-being in the wombs of our hearts and minds. We must gestate this aspect of ourselves through various stages of growth, and then birth it to be our true self. We are not physical beings who love spirituality; rather, we are celestial beings who are *temporarily* incarnating terrestrially. Therefore, we must rebirth our true, eternal, infinite, spiritual nature.

At this stage the Old Master says that the Heavenly Heart is like the dwelling place and the Light is the master. He further teaches that turning on our inner Light is *not* the *only* requirement; we must *move* the Light. When the Light *moves*, then all the elements of our body and earthy mind redirect their attention *inward*.

> Therefore, you only have to make the Light circulate: that is the deepest and most wonderful secret. The Light is easy to move, but difficult to fix. If it is made to circulate long enough, then it crystallizes itself; that is the natural spirit-body. This crystallized spirit is formed beyond the nine heavens. It is the condition of which it is said in the *Book of the Seal of the Heart*: "Silently in the morning thou fliest upward."[35]

The phrase "thou fliest upward" is King James Bible English creeping into Baynes's translation, because Baynes would have considered such to be *sacred* wording. This phrase could easily be translated, "you fly upward." Cleary translated this: "soaring upward."

When the Old Master refers to the *Book of the Seal of the Heart*, he may be referring to the Jade Emperor's *Mind Seal* book, which I have mentioned previously as a helpful complement to our study, and a text that will be quoted when appropriate. The *Mind Seal* is a Taoist text on how to achieve immortality. Stuart Olsen is the translator and commentator in the English version available on Amazon.com and elsewhere.

Now let's review the actual teaching. Here the master tells us that "the deepest and most wonderful secret" is *moving* the light—referred to as *circulating the light*. This is done using the inhalations and exhalations of our breath with our mind's *imaginative forces*. Cayce uses the term "imaginative forces" to describe that which *moves* us to higher realms: "Unless the inner self is attuned to Creative Forces, or Energies, [these abilities] may be soon entirely forgotten and the abilities to use the imaginative forces . . . will not be the best for the entity."[36] We can't allow our imaginative forces to stagnate, for we could possibly lose them. Imagination is an important aspect of human consciousness for it is capable of expanding our awareness beyond this limited reality we currently live in. Imaginatively visualizing movement within us is key to actually achieving that movement.

The breathing technique associated with this movement may seem to be an odd and unnatural breathing process, but it is very effective. It has given me personally more illumination and revitalization than most any other technique. Remember, it is both mental and physical. Here's how it is done:

Sit in a comfortable position with loose clothing and as much quiet as you can find. Notice the rhythm of your *natural* breathing pattern. Once you are clearly aware of your natural pattern, take hold of your breathing and as you inhale *imagine* yourself drawing energy up from the lower portions of your body, lower chakras, up through your spinal column to your brain stem and then on into your full brain, including your large front lobe (which only humans have, as none of the great apes have a large frontal lobe). You simply imagine or actually feel this energy rising as you inhale. Hold the breath in your brain for a moment. Now imagine the Light, the Heavenly Heart, joining with your raised breath through your crown chakra (your fontanelle or "soft spot" as a baby). You may also find this light in your frontal lobe and pituitary gland (the master gland of the human body). Imagining or feeling union with the Light gives you the *essence* of life itself. Next, exhale *slowly* as you imagine this raised and revitalized energy *bathing* your body as it flows downward again through your lungs, heart, liver, and kidneys to the lower chakras, lower portions. Now, rest in the emptiness of the empty breath, for this is a very still condition. Of course, this will take practice before you can fully control your diaphragm, and thereby control your breath. Repeat this rising and bathing cycle at least three times, up to seven times. Don't do it fast or you may hyperventilate. The more you practice, the easier you can control your breath and move the energy in a circular motion. At first you need to use your imaginative visualization, but eventually you'll actually feel the energy moving. At the crown you'll actually feel a union with the Light, the Heavenly Heart, the Breath of Life. When empty of breath you'll have so much control that you can easily sit still without taking another breath right away. Your body comes to know that you will indeed take another breath, so it relaxes during the empty stillness. See illustration of Circulation of the Light, with energy and breath, on page 4.

Think of the rising portion of this breath cycle as the form of a king cobra in the raised, striking position. It is the ancient *kundalini*, or life force in our bodies. In the *Yoga Sutra* by Patanjali (compiled prior to 400 CE), this pathway is called the *sushumna*, (*sus-shum-na*) with *ida* and *pingala* (*eeda, ping-ala*) weaving around the sushumna. You can see this arrangement in the modern medical profession's *caduceus* symbol (see illustration of the Yoga pathways p. 11.) The sushumna correlates to our central nervous system—our cerebrospinal system (brain and spinal column). Ida and pingala correlate to the twins known as the sympathetic and parasympathetic subsystems of our autonomic nervous system.

Let's return to the original text and the topic of gathering thoughts. See the illustrations of the four stages of this Taoist meditation process on pages 14–17.

> In carrying out this fundamental principle you need to seek for no other methods, but must only concentrate your thoughts on it. The book *Leng Yen* says: "By collecting the thoughts one can fly and will be born in heaven." Heaven is not the wide blue sky, but the place where corporeality [the physical portion of our being] is begotten in the house of the Creative. If one keeps this up for a long time, there develops quite naturally, in addition to the body, yet another spirit-body.

The reference to the book *Leng Yen* is likely to the *Leng Yen King*, which was translated by Hindu–Buddhist monk Paramiti in 705 CE. Of course, the original text was of much greater antiquity. It became a sutra of *Sthaviravāda*, literally "Teaching of The Elders," and was the sutra of one of the early Buddhist schools dating around 100 CE. Its original Hindu documents were lost over the ages but were preserved in Chinese and Tibetan literature. As we see in the Old Master's teaching, it contained wisdom about "collecting the thoughts." The text of this document is a discussion between Buddha and Ananda about the location and power of distractions, and how to capture and contain them. The teaching here is that if we practice collecting our thoughts in one location and not concentrating on them for a length of time, then we can be born again into Heaven, "the house of the Creative." Edgar Cayce often spoke of the power of renewal, revivification, and illumination of the *Creative* Forces versus the *destructive* forces, that so often beset us in daily life.

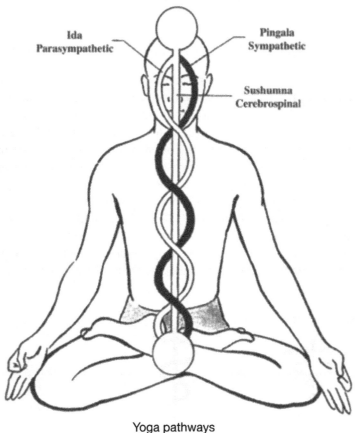

Yoga pathways

An expanded, stylized Caduceus: originally the staff of the Greek god
Hermes Trismegistus (as below left) depicting the cerebrospinal path,
Yoga's Sushumna, the double serpents of the Ida and Pingala as
the Autonomic nervous system, and the circular wheels of the seven
chakras as the endocrine glands. The wings represent the mind's uplifting aid to healing. A simpler version was the staff of Greek healer
Asclepius (center below), who also used a patient's dreams to diagnose
and prescribe. Today, Hermes's staff is a symbol used by doctors, Asclepius's rod is a symbol used by EMTs and ambulances (below center).
Pharmacists use the symbols for *Hygeia,* the Greek goddess of hygiene
(below right, the chalice), and the daughter of Asclepius (below right,
the serpent). The serpent symbolizes the life force in the body.

The Old Master has just taught us that in the womb of the house of the Creative, another body is conceived and grows. It is the spirit-body. Continuing with the Old Master's teachings we find this:

> The Golden Flower is the Elixir of Life (*Chin-tan*; literally *golden ball or golden pill.*) [Cleary translates it as *golden pill.* I actually found it helpful for me to think of it as a *liquid* rather than a pill. An *elixir* filled me with the energy of a *tonic*, spreading throughout my body/mind quicker than a pill.] All changes of spiritual consciousness depend upon the Heart. Here is a secret charm which, although it works very accurately, is yet so fluid that it needs extreme mindfulness and clarity, and complete absorption and tranquility. People without this highest degree of mindfulness and understanding do not find the way to apply the charm; people without this utmost capacity for absorption and tranquility cannot keep fast hold of it.[37]

During my early years of practicing, these words—"highest degree of mindfulness and understanding"—guided me, as did "utmost capacity for concentration and tranquility." However, in all respects I was a typical, young, single, American male. My mind was neither centered nor calm. It churned over everything from yesterday, today, and even *tomorrow*, as well as my inner self-conscious concerns about my place among peers. Sitting in calm, utmost concentration was *not* a condition that came easily to me. From my past lives I did have an *intuitive knowing* of its importance and I could sense how it *should be*, but I needed a lot of training and practice in order to abide in that condition for any length of time. Now, some 50 years later, it has become so natural, so easy, as to be like breathing. I can experience this in the midst of all sorts of commotion—of course, it is always best in a quiet place and time.

The following illustrations are the four stages of Golden Flower meditation.

Stage 1: Gathering the Light

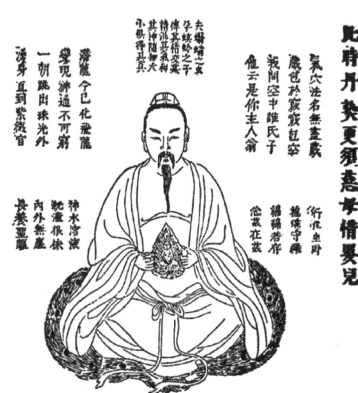

嬰兒現形圖

Stage 2: Origin of a New Being in the Place of Power

Stage 3: Separation of the Spirit-body for Independent Existence.

Stage 4: The Center in the Midst of Conditions

2. The Primordial Spirit and the Conscious Spirit

Duality versus the Singularity, the Three Worlds, the Unmovable Heart, and the Spirit Body

The Old Master said: In comparison with heaven and earth, man is like a mayfly. But compared to the great Way, heaven and earth, too, are like a bubble and a shadow. Only the primal spirit and the true nature overcome time and space.

The *human* mind is possessed by illusions that appear to be very real. The only true reality is what is behind it all. It is both the vital *energy* of life and the *consciousness* of life. It is the *élan vital* that pulses through us. It is a level of consciousness that whispers to us, "there is more to life than this." All reality is an *emanation* from an infinite, creative essence. And this macrocosmic source is also found within of us in microcosm, for we are little universes of beingness that reflect the dynamics of the macrocosm. Each cell in our bodies is a mini–galaxy, with its own "sun" as the *nucleus* and "planets" as the *electrons* circling the nucleus—all of these held together by the so–called "strong and weak forces" and an electromagnetic field. But all of this, the macro and micro, is a *projection* from a *singular* source, and the source is unmoved and eternal.

The source is the only true reality. Becoming conscious of the source changes everything.

Living in this projected reality we see duality: day and night, light and dark, good and evil, me and you, male and female, here and there, suffering and happiness, wisdom and ignorance—the great dualities that compose life in this world. Yet, throughout all of this the secret teaching runs that there is a *oneness*, and that oneness is the *true* spirit and essence of immortal, eternal, infinite life. This is of such importance to our perception that Edgar Cayce felt it was the *first lesson*:

"The first lesson . . . should be ONE—One—One—ONE; Oneness of God, oneness of man's relations, oneness of force, oneness of time, oneness of purpose, ONENESS in every effort—Oneness—Oneness!"[38]

The *samsara* cycle of birth, life, death, and rebirth to which life in the material world is bound, is resolved in the *nirvana/moksha* of a *transcendent* state of consciousness. The transcendent state is the perception of *oneness*.

Time and space are an illusion, a very purposeful illusion, but an illusion, for in the transcendent state there is only one time, one space. In his novel *The Time Machine*, H.G. Wells wrote: "There is no difference between time and any of the three dimensions of space except that our consciousness moves along it." If we rise up from any point on the timeline or spatial formation, we see oneness. Time and space are a condition of consciousness. Edgar Cayce taught: "Time, space, and patience are those channels through which man as a finite mind may become aware of the infinite."[39] To function in the finite realms we need time and space, but patience lifts us into an infinite awareness that sees beyond time and space. Cayce adds a curious role for love in his explanations of time and space: "There is no time, no space, when patience becomes manifested in love. Love unbounded is patience. Love manifested is patience."[40] This type of loving patience overcomes the duality, and the oneness appears quite naturally.

The Old Master teaches that the primal spirit and the true nature overcome time and space. It is the *perception* of the true nature and the *intuitive awareness* of the primal spirit that sees through the illusions.

The energy of the seed, like heaven and earth, is transitory,
but the primal spirit is beyond the polar differences. Here is

the place whence heaven and earth derive their being. When students understand how to grasp the primal spirit, they overcome the polar opposites of light and darkness and tarry no longer in the three worlds.

The three worlds according to Baynes are heaven, earth, and hell. I prefer the three found in so many ancient teachings, such as the Egyptians and Mayans: 1. Heavens, 2. Earth (middle world), and 3. Underworld or Netherworld. In qualities of *perception* or mental states of consciousness they are: 1. transcending consciousness (super-consciousness), 2. physical consciousness, and then, 3. the vast depths of subconsciousness; some call these unconscious realms.

But only he who has envisioned human nature's original face is able to do this.

I remember the first time, after years of seeking, when I reconnected with the womb of all life—what the Old Master called, "human nature's original face." My whole being was supremely content, *finally*. It was truly home, or more accurately, it was "hOMe."

Cayce gave his view of our ultimate purpose for existence: "The purpose is that you might know yourself to be yourself, and yet one with the Creative Forces, or God."[41] This expresses the ancient Hindu concept that despite all appearances to the contrary, our individual soul (*atman*) is *not* separate from the universal creator (*Brahma*). Furthermore, the creator has imbued all souls—yours, mine, and everyone's—with the creative essence or spirit. Many theologies describe the nature of the divine essence as a *trinity*. Let's take a moment to look into this trinity.

The first aspect of God is as the *creator*. This is the motivation that brought all things into existence. The next portion of God is as a *helper* or *savior*, one who lives among the created. And the final aspect is a *mystical quality* of God that is known only through an inner, transcendental awakening and union, often a *re*-union.

In Christianity the triune aspects of God are the Father, the Son (Savior), and the Holy Spirit (or Ghost). Our Father created us, loves us, and seeks to have our conscious love in return. The Father sent his Son to save us from illusions and loneliness by showing us "The Way." The

Holy Spirit is our resource, bringing "all things to our remembrance"—referred to as the "Spirit of Truth" and the "Comforter" in the Gospel of John.[42] It is an unseen *resource* that we may call on and come to know within our hearts and minds.

Though Judaism does not teach a triune God, in the *Book of Formation (Sepher Yetzirah)* of the Kabbalah, it is said: "God created the world through three *seraphim.*" Genesis has God delineated by three names: 1. *Elohim* (translated into English as "God"), who creates light and life, and the *spirit* of humans in its own image; 2. *Yahweh Elohim* (translated into English as "Lord God"), who creates us physically from the dust of the earth, separates us into masculine and feminine, and companions with us in the Garden; and then 3. *Yahweh* (translated into English as "Lord") who interacts with us *after* the loss of the Garden.[43]

In Ancient Egypt, there were several trinities, but one of the most commonly depicted was Ra, Mut, and Amon Ra. Ra (pronounced *ray*) is the source of all life and each life is a ray from this great ray. Mut is the mother and nurturer that actively cares for us. And Amon Ra is the *hidden* aspect of God, the unseen source of health, harmony, fertility, and the goodness of all things. You can quickly see how this is Father, Mother, and hidden Spirit, and reflects three aspects of the Divine.

In Hinduism, we find the trinity portrayed in Brahma, Vishnu, and Shiva. Brahma is the creator (*Svayambhu*, meaning "self-born"), Vishnu is the preserver, and Shiva is the destroyer (of ignorance and illusions). Brahma put its eternal spirit into all of creation. The eternal spirit takes no form but is expressed by the life *in any form*. The individual spirit of a creature is always connected to the original, omnipresent, eternal spirit. Brahma is depicted with four heads and hands. The four heads face all directions. The four hands contain a water bottle (symbol of life), prayer beads (symbol of devotion), the Vedas (symbol of knowledge), and a creation tool (*sruva*, a symbol of his role as a *creative* force). Vishnu is depicted with one head, which is surrounded by several (often seven) flared cobra heads—symbolizing his powerful kundalini energy. In his four hands are a conch shell, indicating the spread of the divine sound *OM*; a spinning disk of light representing a chakra and the wheel of time; a lotus, indicating enlightenment; and the mace of lordship, indicating his role as the "preserver" or savior. Shiva is most often depicted in meditation with the water of life coming out of his topknot and running upward to a high mountain, representing the source of original life. A third eye on his forehead conveys his deeper sight. His eyes are often half closed revealing his inner focus. His body is covered in ashes, symbolizing life *beyond* death. A moon crescent is seen near his head, and the radiant sun surrounds his head like a halo, revealing his ability to be in the source of all light (the sun) and to reflect that light when in darkness (the moon).

In Taoism, God can be understood through *San Qing* (*Q* is pronounced as *ch*, so *ching*, rhymes with *sing*), which refers to the three pure heavens and three pure aspects of God: 1. *Yu Qing* is the Jade Pure aspect of the infinite one and is the creator of Heaven and Earth. In this aspect is *Yuanshi Tianzun*, also *Yuan-shi tian-zong*, said to be without beginning and the most supreme of all beings; in fact, it represents the principle of being and is the prototype of a being. From him all things arose. He is eternal, limitless, and invisible. However, he desired to withdraw from active participation in the unfolding of creation, so he took on an apprentice, the Jade Emperor, who is the ruler of the universe using universal laws. 2. *Shang Qing* is the Upper Pure aspect of the one God and is *Lingbao Tianzun*, also *Ling-bao tian-zong*, sometimes called *Dao-Jun*, "Lord of the Way," and *Tian-shang dao-jun*, "Supreme Master of the Way." He is considered to be the guardian of magical writings (*Ling-bao jing*). He has existed since the beginning of the physicality, and it is his task to calculate time, allocate it to the various epochs, and to regulate *yin* and *yang*. 3. The third aspect of the trinity is *Tai Qing*, the Great Pure, and is also known as *Daode Tianzun*. He represents the immortal and divine teacher. He will assume a great variety of forms to bring the people of the "world of dust" closer to the teachings of the Tao.

Trinity is not an expression of multiple gods but an attempt to render the one, ineffable God in three understandable *roles*. These three are meant to help our three-dimensional nature better comprehend God and our relationship with the Divinity.

Like an ember, these truths lie quietly within us waiting to be fanned into a sacred fire that reawakens our celestial nature.

> When men [i.e., humans: men *and* women] are set free
> from the womb, the primal spirit dwells in the square inch
> [between the eyes in the center of the brain], but the

conscious spirit dwells below in the heart. [Our spiritual
nature is in the higher chakras in the brain of the body
temple, while our outer, conscious self is in the heart
chakra.] This lower fleshly heart has the shape of a large
peach: it is covered by the wings of the lungs, supported by
the liver, and served by the bowels. This heart is dependent
on the outside world. If a man does not eat for one day even,
it feels extremely uncomfortable. If it hears something terrify-
ing it throbs; if it hears something enraging it stops; if it is
faced with death it becomes sad; if it sees something beautiful it is dazzled. But the Heavenly Heart in the head, when
would it have been moved in the least? Dost thou ask: Can
the heavenly heart not move? Then I answer: How could the
true thought in the square inch move? If it really moves, that is
not good. For when ordinary men die, then it moves, but that
is not good. It is best indeed if the Light has already fortified
into a spirit-body and its life-energy gradually penetrated the
instincts and movements. But that is a secret which has not
been revealed for thousands of years.

When the life force penetrates our earthly instincts and movements,
then our spiritual nature lives. In this passage the teacher begins to
reveal how important it is for us to conceive, nourish, and abide more
in our *spirit* body, while using the *physical* body as a vehicle, a vessel.

The lower heart moves like a strong, powerful commander
who despises the heavenly ruler because of his weakness,
and has usurped the leadership in affairs of state. But when
the primal castle can be fortified and defended, then it is as
if a strong and wise ruler sat upon the throne. The eyes start
the light circulating like two ministers at the right and left who
support the ruler with all their might. When the ruler in the
center is thus in order, all those rebellious heroes will present
themselves with lances reversed ready to take orders.

Here the Old Master uses an allegory to convey the conflict between
the fleshly heart and the Heavenly Heart, and the eventual unification

of them. The earthly body and the outer world can be of such a focus and playground for our lower nature, our mortal, self-seeking nature, that we consider our spiritual being to be too ethereal and misty, weak and useless. A war between these two aspects of our being may develop. But when the powerful lower self surrenders its dominant position and seeks the Heavenly Heart, then the castle can be fortified with the Light and the deadly, rebellious energy ceases its assault, allowing the Light to rule wisely. The proper order of power and truth needs to be established. Cayce taught: "Don't put the material first, for you have to live with yourself a long, long while! Become acquainted with yourself. Know yourself and the relationship to the Creative Forces."[44]

The Problem with "Anima" and "Animus"

In Richard Wilhelm's translation, he used the Jungian terms *anima* and *animus* to convey the Old Master's teachings about yin and yang, the dual nature of consciousness and life. The problem with this is how it taints the feminine as dark, lusty, and the lower nature. Jung taught that anima is the sensual and relational dynamic while animus is the rational and reasoning portion. He wrote, "Woman's psychology is founded on the principle of Eros, the great binder and loosener, whereas from ancient times the ruling principle ascribed to man is Logos."[45] In that statement anima became something other than yin. The use of the feminine as the principle of eros is an *earthy* view of the feminine. In Gnosticism the feminine's higher nature was called, "Wisdom from Above" (*he ano Sophia*). In her ideal essence the feminine is the "Lightsome Mother" (*he Meter he Photeine*). Even in the Holy Bible the first word used to describe the feminine is *chavah*, Hebrew for "life giver" (Genesis 3:20, pronounced *kah'-vah*). Terms that demean the feminine are narrow, earthy prejudices and miss the higher qualities of the feminine. We have to be careful about tagging the feminine nature as the dark or lower nature, or as evil, and the bane of good men.

Richard Wilhelm's translation prejudices the masculine and feminine as the brightness versus the darkness. This is a failing of a duality view of life. And this failing becomes extreme in the teaching that the animus and anima part ways after death, with the animus (associated with the *hun*) ascending to higher consciousness (as the *shen*) while the anima (associated with p'o) sinks into darkness because it is "heavy and turbid" and "clings to the body and fleshy heart." Some depth-psychologists believe the anima is not a transcendent being and is tied to this outer life. Wilhelm's association of *hun* and *shen* with animus and p'o with yin misleads us and generates a prejudice in our understanding of male and female. Only a divided mind would perceive this. Duality is an illusion, oneness is the ultimate reality, and is depicted perfectly in the classic yin/yang symbol—the two are aspects of a whole, not separate, not divided, not higher and lower beings. I have changed Wilhelm's translation to convey this united view. Yin and yang, hun and p'o are aspects of *every* soul, *every* psyche, regardless of what gender they are manifesting during this incarnation. See my version of the yin-yang diagram, compared to Wilhelm-Jung's on page 28.

However, Cleary's "lower soul" and "higher soul" doesn't settle with my experiences either because the soul is one singular entity. I'm using "lower nature" and "higher nature" to describe the forces at play within *every* soul. Also, instead of indicating that lower nature is "feminine" as Wilhelm did, I'm using Cleary's description of this as "the dim" awareness, which is natural to our lower nature. Many Taoist teachers believe that the only way to full spirituality is to totally eradicate p'o energy, lower nature, human nature; requiring us to be pure yang, pure hun. This is a misconception due to a dualistic view of reality and eternity. Union (Yoga) of all aspects of our being in the proper balance is the ultimate reality, the ultimate goal. Nothing in eternity is lost; it's either seen/manifested or it is unseen/unmanifested. Therefore, bringing all into coordinated, cooperative balance is the higher truth.

From my years of study and practice using the Cayce teachings and the wiser ancient teachings (especially Gnosticism and Kabbalah), I found my lower nature to be better associated with the "little I am" while my higher nature was in the image of the "Great I AM," who gave us a portion of itself. Furthermore, I like the ancient Egyptian teachings about how our greater power comes when the lower self, or ruler of lower Egypt, and the higher self, or ruler of upper Egypt, work *united* in our search for enlightenment. When our lower self makes time to study and practice concepts that awaken and nourish our higher self, then the higher self awakens. When our lower self uses its will to subdue desires of personal gratification and exaltation for the greater purpose of soul growth, then the higher self awakens. Here is where the whole teaching comes together in the yin–yang union—with a little of the yin in our yang, and a little of the yang in our yin, and the united symbol of the two working as one. This is Cayce's "one, one, one" teaching. The yin–yang symbol is a union of these two, working together for a higher goal.

Before I leave this gender prejudice I have to share an overlooked teaching from *original* Taoism. That is, the teaching about the "Dark Depth Female" or the "Mysterious Female," 玄牝 (*hsüan pìn /xuán pìn*). Here "dark" clearly means hidden, unseen; not evil or "heavy" or "turbid." She is in fact the *gateway."* At the dark depth of this Dark Depth, lies the gateway to the various surprises of Tao." The act of remembering is the secret, called "the attainment of Dark Depth"—玄德 / 得 (*hsüan te/ xuán dê*). Her magic is in the action that leads to inaction, the being that leads to nonbeing.[46] Russian sinologist, Evgueni A. Tortchinov, wrote extensively about this doctrine of the "Mysterious Female."[47] Here's an excerpt: "The principal purpose of this paper is to suggest the approach of transpersonal psychology for analysis of some important aspects of the Taoist doctrine, that is, the concept of the Tao as *a female universal principle."* Tortchinov adds that the Taoist feminine principle is "to be like an infant" or even as an "embryo." Remember, Jesus also touched on this: "Truly I tell you, unless you change and become like little children, you will never enter the kingdom of heaven. Therefore, whoever takes the lowly position of this child is the greatest in the kingdom of heaven."[48] Tortchinov wrote: "To understand these Taoist principles, we must begin from the very beginning—from the central concept of Taoism, that is, Tao (the Way, the True Way). The female, maternal image of Tao is the crucial point to understanding the psycho–technique (or psycho-practical) approach of Taoism. It is possible to demonstrate its importance by citing a passage from the *Tao Te Ching*: 'The valley spirit never dies—it is called the mysterious female; the gate of the mysterious female is called the root of heaven and earth.'"

The Dark Depth Female is a state of consciousness, not a being. All seekers must achieve this state in order to transcend. During one of my deep meditations I perceived and blended with what felt to be the womb of "Mother God." It felt like my original home, or "hOMe." To me this was the Dark Depth Female, and was the gateway to enlightenment.

While in this state of being, I was "touched." The touch changed me forever. Even when my humanness rose again, there remained a spark in me that had not be there before. Sometimes I simply have to close my eyes and there is that womb of my origin, that intimate umbilical connection with Mother, the Life Giver—all my human nature falls away and I am pure again. Of course, there is still much to do in this incarnation, so I return to my human nature and struggle to do my best.

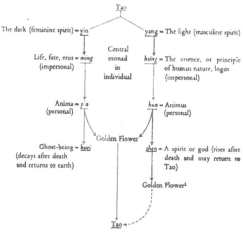

This is the original diagram in the Wilhelm-Jung book.
Below is my version.

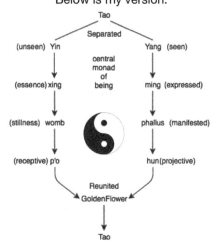

Here is the next teaching from the Old Master without any gender prejudice:

> The way to the Elixir of Life known as supreme magic is seed-water, spirit-fire, and thought-earth; these three. What is seed-water? It is the true, one energy of former heaven. Spirit-fire is the light. Thought-earth is the heavenly heart of the middle dwelling. Spirit-fire is used for effecting, thought-earth for substance, and seed-water for the foundation. Ordinary people make their bodies through thoughts ["As a person thinks in the heart, so is he/she." Proverbs 23:7]. The body is not only the seven-foot-tall outer body. In the body is the lower nature. The lower nature adheres to consciousness, in order to affect it. Consciousness depends for its origin on the lower nature. [Here we may consider the lower nature's *will to survive* as among its fundamental motivations; thus, keeping consciousness conscious.] Lower nature is dim, it is the substance of consciousness. As long as this consciousness is not interrupted, it continues to beget from generation to generation, and the changes of form of the lower nature and the transformations of substance are unceasing. [This is referring to the seemingly bottomless wheel of the lower self's birth, life, death, and rebirth—reincarnation and karma—a process affecting our souls from generation to generation, until liberation is achieved.]

There comes a point in everyone's life when they pause and say, "this can't be all there is to life!" When that point is reached, the lower nature begins to seek the higher nature and give space for the higher view, the higher nature.

> But, besides this, there is the higher nature in which the spirit shelters. The higher nature lives in the daytime in the eyes; at night it houses in the liver. When living in the eyes, it sees; when housed in the liver, it dreams. Dreams are the wanderings of the spirit through all nine heavens and all the

nine earths. But whoever is in a dark and withdrawn mood
on waking, and chained to his bodily form, is fettered by
the lower nature. Therefore, the concentration of the higher
nature is affected by the circulation of the light, and in this
way the spirit is maintained, the lower nature subjugated, and
[its] consciousness cut off.

When the lower nature wearies of its selfish journey, it opens itself
to the way of the higher nature. It actually subjugates its desires and
habit patterns to allow for a change in consciousness and motivation.
Cayce associated this change with the crucifixion that transformed Jesus
Christ into the resurrected one: "Crucify desire in self, that you may be
awakened to the real abilities of helpfulness that lie within your grasp."[49]
When our lower nature reaches that point where it wants more out
of life than just to live it, it makes room for the higher self, the higher
motivations.

In this next passage we have some very helpful information in the
form of the magical three components of the Elixir of Life: 1. seed–water,
which is the origin of our vital energy; 2. spirit–fire, which is the origin
of our higher consciousness; and, 3. thought–earth, which is the means
to *individuation*, or *personal* awareness. When the self–conscious nature
is fully expressed, the vital energy and original consciousness live in
the so–called *unconscious*. The self–seeking, self–gratifying portion lives
in physicality as a separate being encased inside a temporary body.
It attempts to maintain the personal consciousness at the expense of
the original, universal consciousness. However, like the beetle's seed
inside the dung ball (body), the original oneness is inside the illusory,
temporary, seemingly separate self. When the outer, separated self longs
for greater meaning and seeks *within* its heart and mind, then the Light
begins to circulate and the seed heats up, ultimately reaching the point
of rebirth.

The method used by the ancients for escaping from the
world consisted in melting out completely the slag of darkness [illusion] in order to return to the purely creative. This
is nothing more than a reduction of the lower nature and a
completion of the higher nature. And the circulation of the

> Light is the magical means of reducing the dark, and gaining mastery over the lower nature. Even if the work is not directed toward bringing back the Creative, but confines itself to the magical means of the circulation of the light, it is just the light that is the Creative. By means of its circulation, one returns to the Creative. If this method is followed, plenty of seed-water will be present of itself; the spirit-fire will be ignited, and the thought-earth will solidify and crystallize. And thus the holy fruit matures. The scarab rolls his ball and in the ball there develops life as the effect of the undivided effort of his spiritual concentration. If now an embryo can grow in manure, and shed its shells, why should not the dwelling place of our heavenly heart also be able to create a body if we concentrate the spirit upon it?

Here we see how similar teachings were around the whole ancient world. It was a period when we, as incarnating celestial beings, were new to incarnating into this physical world. For example, the Chinese master used a metaphor that also belonged to ancient Egyptian mystical teachings—that is the dung beetle and the scarab, as symbols of rebirth from out of the dung of life.

The *Real* Yin and Yang

In the lessons to come there is again a gender prejudice in the translation. It expresses the longstanding bias against the female as being the temptress that brings down humanity. It is simply not true and it wasn't true in the purest of ancient wisdom to come down to us. The higher understanding knows that the feminine spirit has a *divine* aspect as well as an earthy side. Unfortunately, the translation only sees her as earthy. The *yin* is interpreted as darkness in the sense of sensuous pleasure, blood, and death. The greater truth is that the darkness of the yin is not the darkness of evil but of the unseen, hidden, and inner realms. Nature has made the female body with its wonders *inside* its form. Unlike the outer phallus and upper-body muscles of the male, the female has *inner* features: vagina, womb, and mammary glands. She cycles like the moon with her menstruation; she conceives life *within* herself; gestates life *within* herself; and even when that life is born, she nourishes it from *within* her breasts. Breast milk was known as "white blood." This is because it is a living substance that contains enzymes, antibodies, and white blood cells (the cells that fight infection).

In the biblical book of the Revelation we see two sides of the feminine clearly depicted in the characters of the Whore of Babylon and the Divine Feminine.[50] The Whore gets most of the attention, but the Divine Feminine is so very important in the vision of John and the archangel Michael who helps here. She is described as standing on the moon, wrapped in the sun, with 12 stars over her head, and pregnant. She eventually births the divine child with the help of Michael who drives evil away from her in order for the new birth to occur without harm. Each psyche has an earthy whore-like quality as well as a heavenly life-giving quality. We men can think of this as our whoremongering desire for sex without love or care versus our higher manly role as lover, protector, and provider. It's helpful to note that when we struggle with these opposing urges, we have heavenly help from the angels—as did John when Michael appeared and helped him.

Yin and yang are *equals* in a complementing, balanced wholeness of being, *both* having a lower nature and a higher one. I have adjusted Wilhelm's translation accordingly in the following lessons.

> The one effective, true human nature, when it descends into the house of the Creative, divides into higher nature and lower nature. The higher nature is in the Heavenly Heart. It is of the nature of light; it is the power of lightness and purity. It is that which we have received from the great emptiness, that which is identical in form with the primordial beginning.

Stop for a moment and reflect on the implications in this last line: "It is that which we have received from the great emptiness, that which is identical in form with the primordial beginning." These words may expand our consciousness. We received the light from the vast, infinite source of our creation: "the great emptiness." We might think of this as an infinite consciousness that is perfectly still—nothing has been conceived. It is empty but with all the potential to conceive—like any consciousness that is still. Then, within this infinite mind it began to move and conceive of what we have come to call "the creation." We were among the many wonders that the infinite mind conceived, giving us the light of consciousness.

Now the Old Master is telling us that this is identical in form with our *primordial beginning*—that portion of us existing from the beginning. This is not a new teaching, but it is often a forgotten one and is certainly a paradoxical one. Surprisingly, Jesus taught Nicodemus that, "No one has ascended up to heaven, who did not *first come down from heaven, even the son of man which is in heaven.*"[51] Despite all of our feelings to the contrary, we were and are heavenly, celestial beings temporarily incarnating in this world. At the Last Supper Jesus tells his disciples that they *already know where he is going*—because deep within them is the celestial portion of their being. Of course, Thomas doesn't understand this, stating that they do *not* know where Jesus is going. Philip then asks Jesus to *show* them, to which Jesus attempts to convey how the "kingdom of God is within you,"[52] by saying, "Have I been with you so long, and yet you do not know me, Philip? He who has seen me has seen the Father [the *Heavenly* Father]; how can you say, 'Show us the Father'? Do you not believe that I am in the Father and the Father in me? The words that I say to you I do not speak on my own authority; but the Father who dwells in me does his works. Believe me that I am in the Father and the Father in me; or else believe me for the sake of the works themselves."[53]

The Old Master's teaching that a portion of our present being is identical to our nature *before* time began is a paradox to our lower, three-dimensional minds. When Cayce taught, "there is no time in spirit," he meant it. Our spirit nature is eternal, timeless. Consider Cayce's reading for his friend Mr. "877" (for privacy, names were replaced with numbers). His friend asked if he and his friend Edgar Cayce had a relationship in a past life, to which the trance-state Cayce replied that the period being discussed in the present reading of the Akashic record was *500,000 years before even the Law of One entered the world!* (877-26, my emphasis) The "Law of One" was a soul group that held that despite appearances to the contrary, there was a universal oneness. It is difficult for our three-dimensional minds to comprehend a relationship 500,000 years *before* we ever came to this planet; it boggles the lower mind! But it helps if we think of ourselves in a different condition than we experience today—here's Cayce again: "Individuals *in the beginning* were more of thought forms than individual entities with personalities as seen in the present."[54] I find it much easier to accept our existence as soul-minds without bodies prior to ever coming to Earth, somehow that settles well with me. I can *intuitively* feel myself beyond my physical body—a spirit-consciousness. In deep meditation this is much easier to perceive as being true. I've often felt that when my body physically dies, the transition will be as familiar as my experiences in deep meditation. The inner me will simply assume central consciousness as it does during deep meditation.

Let's continue with the Old Master:

> The lower nature partakes of the nature of darkness. It is the energy of the heavy and the turbid [the condition of matter versus pure spirit]; it is bound to the bodily, fleshly heart. The higher nature loves life. The lower nature seeks death. [Here we may think of "death" in the sense of the menstrual cycle, cycles of the moon, and/or the ever-changing nature of temporal life. More on this in a moment.] All sensuous desires and impulses to anger are effects of the lower nature; it is the conscious spirit which after death is nourished on blood, but which, during life, is in great distress.

This association with blood is among the mystery teachings of the ancient world. The word "sacrifice" is composed of two Latin words meaning "to make sacred." Around the ancient world and in most all ancient religious practices, shedding blood was considered to be the way to make the profane holy again. This idea comes from the belief that the spirits of the so-called "Children of God" chose flesh over spirit because it allowed them complete self-expression and self-gratification in a sensuously stimulating flesh body. Thus, returning to the spirit, or pure energy, required shedding the blood of the physical form. Often this was done by killing and offering up an animal, but in some cultures it included human sacrifice. Even in Judeo-Christian lore, it was secretly held that a messiah, a savior would have to offer up his blood as a sacrifice that would take away the "original sin" of seeking self-gratification over spiritual oneness. This was also known to be the meaning behind the curse of Eve and all women, by shedding their blood in order to cleanse their wombs for a potential birth of new life. The hormonal changes prepare the uterus for pregnancy when blood and tissue lining the uterus (womb) break down and leave the body. Then, the body is prepared for pregnancy each month when one of the ovaries releases an egg (ovulation). This cycle reflects the process of blood cleansing in preparation for conceiving new life in a purified womb. On the soul level, this represents the shedding of the blood of earthiness and selfishness in order to prepare the womb of our minds and hearts for spiritual conception and pregnancy. It was also believed that the blood cleanses from all sin, all unrighteousness, and was stated by the disciples John and Paul: "If we walk in the light, as he is in the light, we have fellowship with one another, and the blood of Jesus his Son cleanses us from all sin."[55]

Next, the Old Master teaches us that we have the latent ability to "distill" the lower nature completely and transform ourselves into pure light! Wilhelm's and Bates's use of the word "distill" is so appropriate to this particular process. Distillation is a process to *purify* by *vaporizing*. Cayce describes deep meditative transitions as moving from solid (ice) to liquid (water) and then to gaseous (vaporous) conditions by stimulating the vibrations of our solid bodies (ice) with the heat generated by reversing the flow of the life force, thus becoming *fluid* (water), and, when heated further, becoming as expansive as a cloud (vapor).[56]

Cleary's translation adds to this, saying: It "is a means of controlling the lower soul, which is a means of interrupting consciousness." Interrupting the constant consciousness of the lower nature for periods of reflection, meditation, and intuitive perception is a significant portion of the enlightenment process. Cleary continued: "Turning the light around is the secret of dissolving darkness and controlling the lower soul. There is no exercise to restore the creative, only the secret of turning the light around. The light itself is the creative; to turn it around is to restore it."

Here is the Old Master's teaching about this:

> Darkness returns to darkness and like things attract each
> other according to their kind. But the pupil understands how

> to distill the dark lower nature completely so that it transforms
> itself into pure light.

Cayce taught that meditation is actual creation taking place, so purification and centering is critical to success. Cayce: "Find that which is
to *yourself* the more certain way to your consciousness of *purifying* body
and mind, before you attempt to enter into the meditation as to raise
the image of that through which you are seeking to know the will or the
activity of the Creative Forces; for you are *raising* in meditation actual
creation taking place within the inner self!"[57]

In the following we again have Wilhelm's use of the terms anima
and animus, and the perpetuation of a sexist prejudice that taints the
feminine as weak, earthy, and the devil's temptress. Much of this comes
from a misunderstanding of the Garden of Eden story, where it appears
that Eve is the first to disobey God and then tempts Adam into sin.

Here's an alternative view:

Original Sin

First, we have to understand that from Cayce's reading of the Akashic
record, Adam was not just an individual but represented an entire *soul
group*. The parentheses in this discourse were Cayce's actual side comments. His life-long stenographer, Gladys Davis, explained that while
giving a reading he would often pause and give her a side comment
which she would put into parentheses: "Man, in Adam (as a group; not
as an individual), entered into the world (for he entered in five places at
once, we see—called Adam in one, see?), and as man's concept became to
that point wherein man walked not after the ways of the Spirit but after
the desires of the flesh *sin* entered—that is, away from the Face of the
Maker, see? and death then became man's portion, *spiritually*, see?"[58]

His mention of "five places" was a reference to his teaching about
the five races of humanity originating in five specific locations on the
planet simultaneously. The yellow race was in the Gobi (but it was
then a lush place unlike the desert that it is today), the white in the
Caucasus Mountains (as in "Caucasian"), the red in legendary Atlantis
and the Americas, the brown in the Andes mountains, and the black in
the plain and Sudan of Africa. Cayce explained that this division was a

natural result of the descent from celestial oneness into the elements of the physical realms and the five senses that function here. Each of the five groups had a special ability to spiritualize one of the five senses that possess human nature: yellow was hearing, white was sight, red was touch, brown was smell (scent), black was taste. Ultimately, the five groups would reunite into one, each bringing the benefit from their mastery of one of the senses.

Traditionally, the sin of Adam and Eve is seen as disobedience—eating the forbidden fruit of the Tree of the Knowledge of Good and Evil. They and the soul group wanted to use their free wills as they pleased, even if it was out of harmony with God's will. Cayce teaches over and over the need to harmonize our free will with God's will if we are to have the greater awakening. In psychological terms, Carl Jung considers Adam and Eve's original sin to correspond to the splitting off of the *outer* consciousness from the *inner* unconscious.[59] Kabbalah takes a little deeper look into Original Sin, and finds more than disobedience. Let's take a moment to explore the Kabbalah view further.

In the Garden of Eden, after eating from the Tree of the Knowledge of Good and Evil, Adam and Eve, attempted to *hide* from God because they felt naked or exposed to the All-knowing Consciousness. There was no real way to hide from the All-Knowing, yet, out of love for us, God created the illusion of time and space, giving them and us a sense of privacy. In this way they, and we, would feel that we had time to improve and that our imperfections were in a private "space" of our own. Achieving this illusion was done by the creation of a veil between our lower nature and our higher nature. This was symbolized in the Bible story by God making "clothes" for Adam and Eve to cover them and their leaving the Garden of God's immediate presence. Of course, there was no way to actually be outside of the Whole, but one could feel that way because of the veil.

In Kabbalah's *The Zohar*, it is written, "Yahweh Elohim [English: *Lord God*] expelled him from the Garden of Eden . . . He drove out et Adam." (Vol. 1, p. 298) Now there is no interpretation for the Hebrew term *et* because it doesn't really mean anything, yet תא [et] is the most frequent word in Hebrew. It is a *structural word* that tells us something about the grammar of the sentence. The word תא comes before a definite object, such as "Adam." It has no equivalent in the English language—and therefore is difficult to translate. Its odd placement in this passage caused Kabbalists to suspect that there was a secret message here. They came to believe that et was a code term related to the tenth, and final emanation of God in the Tree of Life (see illustration p. 38), and the 10th emanation is *Shekhinah* [pronounced in Hebrew *shu-kee-nuh'* but many say *shek-een-ah'*].

The Shekhinah represents the *presence* of God in this world, but the nuance is that it is the *Feminine Presence* in this world—Mother God or the Divine Feminine, partially associated with "Mother Earth." The feminine expression was a gift from God (Genesis 2:22) to allay the loneliness that occurs in this world of separation (Genesis 2:18). The illusion of separate, individual privacy required a conscious loss of oneness. The truth of oneness now lay on the other side of the veil, in our higher nature.

The Kabbalah's Deeper Mystical Version of the Tree of Life
Notice "The Deep," that is the Way to the Origin

Let's review two more passages in Genesis. In Genesis 2:21 God cast a magic sleep over the androgynous adam (the word was not a name yet, so it was written in English using a lower case "a" and simply meant "person" or "being"). Once in the deep sleep that God cast over the person (adam), God draws out the *feminine side* (the Hebrew word that was translated "rib" (*tsela*, צ.ל.ע, pronounced *tsay-law*) also means "side," and is used by God to describe the *sides* of the Ark of the Covenant—"rib" is a prejudiced translation of *tsela*). When the now male–only side awakens (Genesis 2:23), now using the proper-named "Adam," he turns to the new being that God separated out, woman. He then says, "She shall be called Woman" (In Hebrew the name is *Ishshah*, אשה—literally *she-man*, meaning "the being with the womb"—see Adam Clarke's *Commentary on the Holy Bible*, 1832). A bit later in Genesis 3:20 it is written, "And Adam called his wife's name Eve; because she was the mother of all living." In Hebrew his wife's name was *Chavvah* (ה.ו.ה—but it was transliterated to Eve). Chavvah literally means "life-giver," and with an initial capital "C" it becomes a proper name in English. This passage indicates that woman is a physical expression of the Divine Life–Giver, the God-Mother, the Womb of God now incarnate among us. The feminine was an emanation of God's being created physically as a gift to humanity to allay loneliness.

In Genesis 3:22, the expulsion from the Garden comes right after this curious passage is spoken by Yahweh Elohim: "Behold, the man (literally, "person") has become like one of us (gods, as clearly stated in Psalm 82:6, "You are gods, and all of you are sons [and daughters] of the Most High."), knowing good and evil; and now, lest he put forth his hand and take also of the Tree of Life, and eat, and live forever . . . " Then the passage abruptly ends. It just moves on to the expulsion from the Garden. Why? Living forever on this side of the veil and in this physical world was never part of the creation plan for the Children of God. Our spiritual souls were never meant to live in terrestrial physicality forever; we are destined to be celestial, heavenly godlings with our Creator, forever. Incarnations were to be temporary. They were meant to be opportunities to make new and better choices, resolving karma and gaining wisdom and mastery of free will; just as God taught Cain, the wayward son of Adam and Eve: "Sin lies at the door [of your consciousness] and its desire is for you. *You must master it.*" (Genesis 4:7, my italics).

For Kabbalists, the secret sin was when Adam and the soul group so desired physical expression of the feminine that he and we abandoned our relationship with Heavenly Mother and Father. This strange idea is written in Genesis 6:2: "The sons of God saw the daughters of men that they were fair; and they took for wives all of them that they chose." The children of God (written in masculine–dominant times as "*sons* of God") "divorced" themselves from their spiritual "marriage" to our heavenly source. We turned all our attention and consciousness toward the physically expressed world. And this was not just to appreciate the pleasing beauty and pleasant demeanor of life in physical form, no. The "sons" (male and female) became driven by desire and craving for Mother Earth and sought to take possession of Her for our gratification. This theme is also found in Gnosticism's tale of the capture of Sophia, the Divine Wisdom in feminine expression, and the subsequent imprisonment of Her in this lower world. Interestingly, Gnostics also believed that Jesus Christ descended from heaven *and freed Sophia!* Thereby releasing Divine Wisdom (the sacred, feminine Shekhinah) from its bonds to this reality.

Here are two supporting passages about Shekhinah: "When Rav Yosef heard his mother's footsteps, he would say: 'I will arise before Shekhinah who is approaching.'"[60] Notice the correlation between Shekhinah and "mother." And here's another passage: "Happy are the righteous! For they cause Shekhinah to dwell on earth."[61] God brought the feminine into the world (Genesis 2:22) with the help of the righteous. Edgar Cayce: "Are you not all children of God? Are you not co–creators with Him? Have you not been with Him from the beginning?"[62] Souls are co–creators with the Creator, but they pulled away from this relationship.

This separation could not be allowed to go on forever, so the Life Forces brought upon us the cycle of birth, life, death, and rebirth until this "divorce" could be repaired. Genesis 3:24 tells how Cherubim with flaming swords were placed around the Tree of Life, symbolizing how immortality was now withheld from us—thus "death" enters our experience. Thankfully, in the last chapters of the Revelation, the redemption of this sad Genesis situation is realized! It is expressed as a Heavenly Bride marrying a physical groom who has become the "Lamb of God."[63] Finally, after such a long journey, the sons and daughters of God are allowed to eat from the Tree of Life, and thus live forever with their Maker![64] Interestingly, Jesus uses this marriage metaphor in his parable of the bride, the bridegroom, and the 10 virgins with their oil lamps.[65] These 10 emanations, 10 virgins, bride, and bridegroom come from the secret teachings of the Kabbalah. Hmm, was Jesus trained in the Kabbalah?

Keep in mind that what I've just shared is an *archetypal dynamic*, not an individual one. Each individual woman is an individual "son" of God with her own soul dynamics and karmic patterns. But Woman as an archetype is the expression of the Divine Life Giver. Also, in this metaphor Adam does not represent individual men. Adam or "man" represents the strength to do good or evil *with* the Life Giver (Eve) as expressed in physicality. Both women and men, as archetypes and we as individuals, must learn to master selfish free-will urges and desires. Furthermore, each individual woman and man has *conscious and unconscious* dynamics. The unconscious is *behind* the veil. If each is to gain their whole consciousness, they must become aware of the separation and reunite the outer finite self with the inner infinite self, and return to oneness with the Creator, or Creative Forces—the primordial Essence from which all life emanated.

3. Circulation of the Light and Protection of the Center

The Secret Revealed

The Old Master said, Since when has the expression "circulation of the Light" been revealed? It was revealed by the "True Men of the Beginning of Form." ["true humans," for early Taoism had wise female teachers, too] When the light is made to move in a circle, all the energies of heaven and earth, of the light and the dark, are crystallized.

It helps if we begin by thinking of heaven as our *higher mind* and earth as our body temple and physical consciousness.

Crystallization is the process by which a solid—its atoms or molecules—changes into a *highly organized structure*, a *crystal*. Jadeite crystals and Dushan jade have been mined and used in China as far back as 6000 BCE. Crystals maintain a precise *frequency* and are used in watches and computers as piezoelectric resonators. Legend holds that the ancient Atlanteans used crystals to channel solar and stellar radiation for use in their power plants. Here the Old Master reveals how the powers of heaven and earth may be ideally channeled within and through us—we may become micro power plants channeling celestial energies in and through the prism of our body temples with its chakras and our mental lotuses.

> That is what is termed as seed-like thinking, or purification of the energy, or purification of the idea. When one begins to apply this magic it is as if, in the middle of the being, there was a non-being.

The crystal has no power of itself but is a *channel* of energy, focusing it and emitting a precise frequency that vibrates throughout our being. The process of purification is the *circulation* of the light. It's like electricity, its power is in moving, flowing. As the light circulates, we move from finite being to infinite non–being in oneness.

> When in the course of time the work is completed, and beyond the body there is a body, it is as if, in the middle of the non-being, there were being. [Here's the paradox: on the other side of our earthly beingness is our heavenly being, and this is awakened by a period of non–being-ness. It's like dying to the finite, journeying through nonbeing, and then awakened as our heavenly being.] Only after concentrated work of a hundred days will the light be genuine, then only will it become spirit-fire. After a hundred days there develops by itself in the middle of the light a point of the true light-pole. Then suddenly there develops a seed pearl. It is as if man and woman embraced and a conception took place. Then one must be quite still and wait. The circulation of the light is the epoch of fire.

Here the word "epoch" is being used to mean the *beginning* of a new era—and that era is one of fire, which is *spirit*. Throughout many mystical teachings, spirit is equated with fire. Here are three examples from the Bible: "I baptize you with water; but he who is mightier than I is coming . . . he will baptize you with the Holy Spirit and with fire." (John the Baptist, Luke 3:16) "There appeared tongues of fire, distributed and resting on each one of them. And they were all filled with the Holy Spirit." (Acts 2:3–4) "God is a Spirit: and they that worship him must worship in spirit and truth." (a statement by Jesus Christ, John 4:24) This concept that God is a spirit-fire motivated the disciple Paul to write: "God is a consuming fire."[66] In the human body, *metabolism* is the fire, burning calories for energy. Proteins and fats are the long-burning fuels while sugars and carbs are the short burning fuels.

The Old Master teaches that after a hundred days of circulating the light there develops a "light-pole" and a "seed pearl," clearly images reflective of the phallus and the ovum (egg), and the Master develops this analogy using the embrace of a man and a woman that results in conception.

> In the midst of primal transformation, the radiance of the light (*yang-kuang*) is the determining thing. In the physical world it is the sun; in man the eye. The radiation and dissipation of spiritual consciousness is chiefly brought about by this energy when it is directed outward (flows downward). Therefore the Way of the Golden Flower depends wholly on the backward-flowing method [flows upward].
>
> The circulation of the light is not only a circulation of the seed-blossom of the body [the seeds may be the egg and sperm but the blossom is the creative energy *within* them], but it is even a circulation of the true, creative, formative energies [latent *within* the procreative cells]. It is not with a momentary fantasy, but with the exhaustion of the cycle (soul-migrations) [seemingly endless soul wanderings] of all the eons. Therefore, the duration of the breath means a year according to human reckoning and a hundred years measured by the long night of the nine paths (of reincarnations).

Here, I disagree with Wilhelm's associating the nine paths with reincarnations. The number nine (九) is considered to be the highest number in the Chinese number system. 1, 2, 3, 4, 5, 6, 7, 8, 9. The odd numbers 1, 3, 5, 7, 9 are *Yang*. The even numbers 2, 4, 6, 8 are *Yin*. If you add the nine numbers, they equal *nine*: $1 + 2 + 3 + 4 + 5 + 6 + 7 + 8 +$

$9 = 45$, and $4 + 5 = 9$. Nine is understood to be a number for *completion* and the ultimate *sum of the yang and yin* numbers. And since the path to enlightenment may require many more incarnations than nine, it is not so much the number of incarnations but that there are nine *developments* that must completed—despite how many incarnations it takes. They are called the "Three Jewels of Tao," which are *virtues*, each containing three *qualities*, thus totally nine:

1) compassion, kindness, love (Chinese uses a term for these that is related to a mother's parental love.)

2) moderation, simplicity, frugality (Chinese term here is, "to be sparing," and when related to morality it means "simplicity of desires.")

3) humility, meekness, modesty. (The third treasure is a six-character phrase instead of a single word, Chinese 不敢為天下先, *Bugan wei tianxia xian*, "dare not to be first in the world." Instructing one to avoid self-glorification, self-exaltation.)

These are more likely the "nine paths" that the Old Master mentions.

Cleary appears to agree, for he wrote that the three treasures of Taoism are vitality, energy, and spirit, and are the fundamental triad of being—known in Taoist terms as the "three treasures" of human existence.

Despite the view of the three treasures that I just stated, Cleary's interpretation conveys a slightly different meaning to the Old Master's nine paths. Here's is Cleary's interpretation:

> These three stages are in each stage, so there are nine
> stages in one stage. I will expound upon that later; for now
> I will speak of three stages in one.

As you can see, Cleary's interpretation identifies these paths as three "stages" and within each there are three stages, thus nine *stages*. He believes that this concept was derived from extant Buddhist documents that were available at the time of the writing of this Taoist book.[67] Of course, I'm saying nine "developments" and Cleary is simply identifying them as nine "stages."

Now back to Wilhelm's and Baynes's translation:

> After a man [person] has the sound of individualization behind him, he will be born outward according to the circumstances, and until his old age he will never look backward. The energy of the light exhausts itself and trickles away. That brings the nine-fold darkness (of reincarnations) into the world.

Here again we see that Wilhelm identifies the nine-fold darkness with reincarnation. Following my earlier interpretation, the darkness is more likely the *opposite* of the virtues of the nine paths; thus, the nine *vices*, which would oppose the virtues. For example, the opposite of the virtue of compassion may be indifference; of love, hate; and of meekness, arrogance. We may readily understand these as being of the lower human nature versus the higher *divine* nature within all souls. The Western world has seven virtues and seven vices. The virtues are commonly listed as: faith, hope, charity (love), justice, prudence, fortitude, and temperance. The vices are listed as: vanity, envy, anger, sloth (laziness), covetousness, gluttony, and lust.

Let's continue with the Old Master's teaching:

> In the book *Leng Yen*[68] it is said: "By concentrating the thoughts, one can fly; by concentrating the desires, one falls." When a pupil takes little care of his thoughts and much care of his desires, he gets into the path of submersion. Only through contemplation and quietness does true intuition arise; for that, the backward-flowing method is necessary.

Thoughts are so important to our development, yet we pay little attention to them. Cayce insisted that we become more aware of our thoughts and their impact on ourselves and others: "Mind is the builder and that which we think upon may become crimes or miracles. For thoughts are things and as their currents run through the environs of an entity's experience these become barriers or steppingstones, dependent upon the manner in which these are laid as it were. For AS the mental dwells upon these thoughts, so does it give strength, power, to things that do not appear. And thus, does indeed there become that as is so oft given, that faith IS the evidence of things not seen."[69] Cayce also says that thoughts are "just as physical as sticking a pin in the hand!"[70] Our thoughts are real, in every sense of that word, as real as actions, actions that may become crimes or miracles.

If our minds can allow for the possibility that the Omnipotent is conscious of us, and cares about us, then all things truly are possible. Can we allow for the possibility that Jesus's teaching about us being gods of the Most High is true? He said, "You are gods, sons and daughters of the Most High."[71]

In the passage we just read the Old Master states that, "Only through contemplation and quietness does true intuition arise." This is true, and Edgar Cayce has much to add to our understanding of intuition and how it is developed. Here are Cayce's teachings:

"Intuition—the faculty—is so often misunderstood. Psychic forces, psychic development are so often misunderstood. Psychic should be applied rather to the soul mind or soul body, than merely to—as is the more often deduced—the MENTAL activities . . . "[72] From Cayce's point of view, a view from the Universal Consciousness, intuition and psychic development are *not* mental activities. They are *soul* abilities. Cayce states that psychic activities are our soul's ability to bring insights and wisdom into this physical plane.[73] The outer self has little idea of where these insights or knowings come from, but sees their influence in daily life. Intuition and psychic knowing do not come from mental activity but from *a closer proximity to one's soul forces*, soul body. If we seek to grow closer to our soul, we *naturally become more intuitive and psychic*. Cayce was once specifically asked for some training, but the lady who requested this did not expect the answer he gave: "Q: Suggest how the entity may train self in the present to the study and use of this intuitive sense. A: Train intuition? Then, how would you train electricity—save as to how it may be governed! ... Hence, in governing, in guarding, in guiding such forces, such powers that arise or manifest or demonstrate through the activities of the body, keep the body, the mind, the soul, in attune with the spheres of celestial forces, rather than of earthly forces."[74]

Notice how Cayce sees intuition as an *already existing influence*, like electricity. One cannot train intuition because it just is. Just as one cannot train electricity. One can only govern it. This is so difficult to accept when we feel that we currently do not have intuition and need to develop it. What we really need to do is to set up our hearts and minds in a manner that channels our soul's natural ability to *flow through us* and to set up some ideals by which we will *govern our use of intuition.*

Another important teaching in this passage by the Old Master is about the concentration of desires that lead to a fall. Desires are of two motivations, selfish cravings and selfless aspirations. Desires have *energy* to them, therefore they are potent forces within us. When the desires flow from our higher nature, we grow. When the desires flow from our lower nature, we slip into unsatisfying, self-centered loneliness. These lower desires can never be fully satisfying, thus they bring no contentment. The higher desires always bring peace and contentment. What is a higher desire? The greatest is love, for the spirit of love *enlivens* everything and everyone. This type of love is *agape* love with a little sprinkle of *philia* love. In classical Greek philosophy there could not be just one word for love, because love is expressed by various motivations. Let's take a moment to better understand love using Greek concepts developed and taught originally by Plato and Aristotle.[75]

Agape love was translated as *charity* by the monks writing the English-language "King James" version of the Bible. It is a selfless love that seeks no reward, often thought of as "unconditional love," but with the connotation of *universal* love, for it has no directed target for its expression or discrimination in its expression. It is a general state of being loving. It creates a depth of contentment that is not found in any other human endeavor.

Philia love is friendship and brotherly or sisterly love. Aristotle believed that a person can bear goodwill to another for one of three reasons: that they are useful; that they are pleasant; and, above all, that they are good; that is, rational and virtuous. Friendships founded on goodness are associated not only with mutual benefit but also with companionship, dependability, and trust. Plato felt that philia love is born out of a passion for one another's companionship that ripens into a higher level of understanding of oneself, the other, and the world. Real friends, real brothers and sisters, add to our lives and understanding of life. Real friends relate authentically and teach us about the vices and virtues in our character. Good relationships become a touchstone for each of us in our mutual journeys through life.

Eros love is intimate, passionate, sexual love. Greeks considered it to be a madness that resulted from Cupid's arrow striking the heart!

Somewhat along the lines of Sigmund Freud's thinking, Plato felt that eros's passion was behind all forms of love, especially philia love. Eros added the energy needed to truly love. He taught that through eros all come to rise to a higher love. He associated eros love with beauty and the magnetic attraction of beauty. He believed that eros love reminded humans of agape love, that it whispered of a lost love that is even better than sex. In John Keats's poetic "Ode on a Grecian Urn," he wrote the famous line: "Beauty is truth, truth beauty." His meaning was that the beauty of artistic imagery conveys more truth than any other form of human expression. Beauty may at first generate lust but it will eventually lead to a higher virtuous love.

Ludus love is playful, uncommitted love. It involves teasing, flirting, seducing, and casual sex. This type of love is expressed in the musical lyric: "Players only love you when they're playing."[76] The focus is on fun, and sometimes on conquest, with no strings attached. Ludus relationships are casual, undemanding, uncomplicated, but they can be long-lasting. When lasting longer than a flirtation, these types of relationships are often referred to as "friends with benefits." Lacking love, these encounters are considered to be mostly recreational.

Storge (pronouced, store-jay) is familial love, which is a kind of philia pertaining to the love between parents and their children.

Philautia (pronounced phil-la-sha) love is self-love, which can be healthy or unhealthy. Unhealthy self-love is self-conceit, a focus on oneself and one's interests over those of others, and the pursuit of gratification from vanity or egotistical admiration of one's idealized self-image (narcissism). However, there is also healthy self-love. Aristotle taught: "all friendly feelings for others are an extension of man's feelings for himself." This level of self-love requires a degree of self-esteem—confidence in one's own worth or abilities; self-respect.

Throughout the Bible, love is of great importance and has a hidden power. When we think of power, even spiritual power, we rarely think of love. Yet, from Genesis to the Revelation, the Bible indicates that love evokes the highest, most godly of powers and is actually a quality of Creative Forces. Love brings us closest to our true, divine nature —our godly nature. Many biblical passages teach that of all the things a person can learn and do in this world, nothing reflects godliness or divinity more than love—learning to love and be loved.

The two greatest commandments are found in both the Old and New Testaments. The first is found in Deuteronomy 6:5 and Matthew 22:37:

"You shall love the Lord your God with all your heart, and with all your soul, and with all your mind."

The second commandment is found in Leviticus 19:18 and Matthew 22:39:

"You shall love your neighbor as yourself." Here the word "neighbor" is *plesion*, meaning a "close-by person." That certainly expands our understanding of just who is our neighbor. Literally, it could be a stranger at the grocery store. Of course, Jesus's teaching at the Sermon on the Mount was and continues to be perplexing to our human nature:

"You have heard that it was said, 'You shall love your neighbor and hate your enemy.'[77] But I say to you, Love your enemies and pray for those who persecute you, so that you may be sons [daughters] of your Father who is in heaven; for he makes his sun rise on the evil and on the good, and sends rain on the just and on the unjust. For if you love those who love you, what reward have you? Do not even the tax collectors do the same? And if you salute only your brethren, what more are you doing than others? Do not even the Gentiles do the same? You, therefore, must be perfect, as your heavenly Father is perfect."

The disciple Paul's famous statement about love is found in 1 Corinthians 13:13:

"Now abide faith, hope, and love [*agape*], these three; but the greatest of these is love."

Paul describes love beautifully: "Love is patient, love is kind, and is not jealous; love does not brag and is not arrogant, does not act unbecomingly; it does not seek its own, is not provoked, does not take into account a wrong suffered, does not rejoice in unrighteousness, but rejoices with the truth; bears all things, believes all things, hopes all things, endures all things. Love never fails."

Peter's love advice is in 1 Peter 4:8: "Above all things, keep fervent in your love for one another, because love covers a multitude of sins."

John wrote in 1 John 4:7-12: "Beloved, let us love one another, for love is from God; and everyone who loves is born of God and knows God. The one who does not love does not know God, for God is love . . . If we love one another, God abides in us, and His love is perfected in us."

Edgar Cayce gave over 2,000 readings teaching spiritual seekers to live, think, speak, and abide in love. Here are his comments to four different people, all given in one discourse[78]:

"Let the beauty of your joy, in manifesting the light and love as shown in the Christ-Spirit, that makes for the new song in your heart, KEEP you in your DAILY walks of life."

"Let others do as they may, but as for you and your house, you will love the LIVING God. KNOW His love is sufficient to keep you. No matter what may be the trial, His love abides, and He is NOT unmindful of your prayers."

"The beauty of your life rises as a sweet incense before the altar of mercy. Yet it is not sacrifice but peace, grace, and mercy that we would manifest among the children of men. For God is love."

"Keep your paths straight. Know in whom you have believed, as well as in what you believe. For the love as passes understanding CAN, does, and will make your pathway brighter. Keep in that way."

Jesus presented love on levels, identifying the highest love in this often quoted passage: "No greater love has a person, than to give up his or her life for another"[79] — this is *not* literal death, but giving up self's desires in order to aid another. It is thinking more of what another may need than what self may want. Cayce said that Jesus had a secret prayer that he repeated to himself, "Others, Lord, others." This kept the Father's power that flowed through Jesus on the right track—not glorifying himself but revealing the Light and Love that flowed through him—God's love, our Father's and Mother's love. Selfless loving is the ideal—giving, caring without expectation of getting something in return. Yet, this must not be self-destructive. No one could accuse Jesus of being a doormat of self-deprecating love. He often radiated a tough love. Those around Him often needed truth, justice, and a clear position on God's ways, not tolerance or pampering. Jesus cared so much for others that he would not let them remain in their darkness or misunderstandings. Yet, he never condemned them. Rather, he called their mistakes to their attention. He also showed a remarkable sense of their inability to handle the full truth, choosing to be patient: "I have yet many things to say to you, but you cannot bear them now."[80]

Let's return to the Old Master's teaching:

In the *Book of the Secret Correspondences*[81] it is said: 'Release is in the eye.' In the *Simple Questions of the Yellow Ruler*[82] it is said: 'The seed-blossoms of the human body must be concentrated upward in the empty space. This refers to it. Immortality is contained in this sentence and also the overcoming of the world is contained in it. This is the common goal of all religions.

The light is not in the body alone, nor is it only outside the body. [This is a direct teaching from the *Simple Questions of the Yellow River*. It explains that incarnate people are microcosms of the universe. The laws of the universe, of Nature, are also at work *inside* each person. The inner and the outer are influencing health and enlightenment.] Mountains and rivers and the great earth are lit by sun and moon; all that is this light. Therefore, it is not only within the body. Understanding and clarity, perception and enlightenment, and all movements (of the spirit) are likewise this light; therefore, it is not just something outside the body. The light-flower of heaven and earth fills all the thousand spaces. But also the light-flower of the individual body passes through heaven and covers the earth. Therefore, as soon as the light is circulating, heaven and earth, mountains and rivers, are all circulating with it at the same time. To concentrate the seed-flower of the human body above in the eyes, that is the great key of the human body. [The "eyes" here include the inner, mind's eye, or third eye, which is the pineal gland in the center of the brain—a gland that contains rods and cones found in our carnal, physical eyes. Why would such cells compose a gland that is in the dark depths of the brain? It sees beyond normal vision.] Children, take heed! If for a day you do not practice meditation, this light streams out, who knows whither? If you only meditate for a quarter of an hour, by it you can do away with the ten thousand eons and a thousand births.

In this closing comment about meditating each day is a truth that is so very difficult to hold to while living our daily life in this world. I have personally experienced how profoundly my mind and heart fall away when my meditation does not occur. I have also noticed how long it takes me to get back to the level of meditative illumination and vibration after missing meditation. And yet, even today, knowing this, life and self-seeking can take me off of my regular practice. I simply have to make it an integral part of physical life and a day's activity—like cleansing, dressing, nourishing my body, and sleeping. It has to be this way or there will always be something that gets in the way of meditation time. Notice how the Old Master is fully aware of this challenge. He requires no more than 15 minutes of meditation to satisfy our daily need.

The Old Master's comment about the light streaming out to who knows where, is found in Jesus's teachings as well. In his discussion with Nicodemus, Jesus said, "The wind blows wherever it pleases. You hear its sound, but you cannot tell where it comes from or where it is going. *So it is with everyone born of the Spirit.*"[85] The Spirit is comparable to the wind. It is unseen but its presence is felt. That portion of us that was initially born or emanated from the Great Spirit can feel the presence and its movements if we but stay still and perceive it. We have lost touch with our *origin*—where our spirit has come from, to where it is going. Regaining awareness requires time in quietness and attentiveness. This type of reflection does not contain thoughts; it is centering consciousness toward the origin of Light and Life.

All methods end in quietness. This marvellous magic cannot be fathomed.

The Old Master is correct; as physically-manifesting beings we find it nearly impossible to appreciate the value of quietness and stillness. Fortunately, modern medicine is reporting success reducing human stress by using meditation.[84] They have also found that long, slow breaths dampen nerve activity that impacts our blood pressure. Just a few minutes of long, slow breathing and the nerve activity that controls our adrenaline's fight-or-flight response slows down. As a result, our blood vessels relax and widen, and stress declines, and our bodies assume a condition that restores health. There is indeed a physical benefit to quietness and stillness. The Old Master is teaching that there is also a mental and spiritual benefit.[85]

> But when the practice is started, one must press on from the obvious to the profound, from the coarse to the fine. Everything depends on there being no interruption. The beginning and the end of the practice must be one. In between there are cooler and warmer moments, that goes without saying. But the goal must be to reach the vastness of heaven and the depths of the sea, so that all methods seem quite easy and taken for granted. Only then have we mastered it.

Over my years of practice, I've experienced the "cooler and warmer moments." In the early years, technique would take up most of my meditative/reflective time, with only brief flashes of Light and vitality. But as my practiced developed, technique would take very little time and periods in the Light were long and nourishing. When my practice was steady, my dreams and intuition were more vivid and present with me. When my practice waned, a foggy mist would cloud my mind, even when my heart was actively giving to and caring for others—I needed meditative time for the fullness of being. Just 15 brief minutes in reflection/meditation would be enough to nourish and enlighten me. Of course, I enjoyed longer periods. I never wanted too many days to go by without spending at least an hour in deep attunement to the Light. But, as British poet William Wordsworth so correctly observed in his sonnet, "The World Is Too Much with Us," life often overwhelms us and waylays our best intentions. We need renewing moments from this reality, and those breaks need to be *in the Spirit*, in the Light. These are found in uninterrupted quietness.

> All holy men [and many holy Taoist women] have bequeathed this to one another: nothing is possible without contemplation (fan–chao, reflection). When Confucius says: 'Perceiving brings one to the goal'; or when the Buddha calls it: 'The vision of the heart'; or Lao-tse says: 'Inner vision', it is all the same.
> Anyone can talk about reflection, but he cannot master it if he does not know what the word means. What has to be

reversed by reflection is the self-conscious heart which has to direct itself towards that point where the formative spirit is not yet manifest. Within our six-foot body we must strive for the form which existed before the laying down of heaven and earth. If today people sit and meditate only one or two hours, looking only at their own egos, and call this reflection, how can anything come of it?

Key to the Master's teaching is his statement: "direct itself towards that point where the formative spirit is not yet manifest." This is the *essence* of spirit. This is the *source* of the emanation of spirit. This is a challenging part of this process. It is like a death of our personality and physical life. We virtually have to let go of our projected self and its life in order to reach *beyond* self for the essence before self existed. This reaching is not so much a yang–driven seeking, but more a yin–*receptive* yielding. Yes, we use our yang–will to subdue the outer reality, to still the daily mind and bodily distractions, but for the ultimate attunement we need to open to the Infinite, Eternal Source of all life, and become receptive. That requires trust, or at the very least faith. We also have to be seriously honest with ourselves about our motivations and expectations. If we are seeking power and self–exaltation, we'll attract darkness. If are seeking humbly, trusting in the All–Knowing, then we will attract Light and Love. What motivates our practice attracts matching vibrations and consciousness. Since this process is dangerous, we need protection; protection from ourselves and protection from the dark forces that seek to disrupt any channel of Light. We must not be naive about this. We are opening ourselves up to powerful, creative forces that will enter us and imbue us with greater vibrations and consciousness. Discernment of the forces is required. We need protection from the ever–so–cunning and insidious energies of delusion and destruction. When done properly our meditation/reflection should leave us more humble, meek, and patient. We should feel softly revitalized. We should feel serene contentment. If not, then we must reconsider the true motivations of our heart.

Next the Old Master begins teaching specific techniques.

The two founders of Buddhism and Taoism have taught

that one should look at the tip of one's nose. But they did not mean that one should fasten one's thoughts to the tip of the nose. Neither did they mean that, while the eyes were looking at the tip of the nose, the thoughts should be concentrated on the yellow middle. Wherever the eye looks, the heart is directed also.

Jesus taught: "Where your treasure is, there will your heart be also. The lamp of the body is the eye; if therefore your eye be single, your whole body shall be full of light."[86]

How can it be directed at the same time upward (yellow middle), and downward (tip of the nose), or alternatively, so that it is now up, now down? All that means confusing the finger with which one points to the moon with the moon itself.

What then is really meant by this? The expression 'tip of the nose' is very cleverly chosen. The nose must serve the eyes as a guide-line. If one is not guided by the nose, either one opens wide the eyes and looks into the distance, so that the nose is not seen, or the lids shut too much, so that the eyes close, and again the nose is not seen. But when the eyes are opened too wide, one makes the mistake of directing them outward, whereby one is easily distracted. If they are closed too much, one makes the mistake of letting them turn inward, whereby one easily sinks into a dreamy reverie. Only when the eyelids are lowered properly halfway is the tip of the nose seen in just the right way. Therefore, it is taken as a guide-line. The main thing is to lower the eyelids in the right way, and then to allow the light to stream in of itself; without effort, wanting the light to stream in concentratedly. Looking at the tip of the nose serves only as the beginning of the inner concentration, so that the eyes are brought into the right direction for looking, and then are held to the guide-line: after that, one can let it be. That is the way a mason hangs up a plumb-line. As soon as he has hung it up, he guides his work by it without continually bothering himself to look at the plumb-line.

Fixating contemplation is a Buddhist method which has not
by any means been handed down as a secret.

This "end of the nose" technique is very useful in the beginning, because it keeps us from "dreamy reverie" and outer-life distractions. The
key to this technique is to remember that it is actually a holding place
for the untrained mind and the untrained heart. The heart goes where
the eyes go, but the end of the nose is nowhere, so the heart becomes
still and the outer busy mind becomes bored. As a result, they yield
their dominance to the subconscious—and the inner concentration can
now begin. I used this technique for a long time with much success,
but eventually I had gained enough control over my dreamy mind and
searching heart that I could close my eyes completely without going
into undirected reverie. Eventually, this allowed me to move far beyond
the body temple into dimensions of ethereal awareness. But this end-
of-the-nose method is a good one when beginning the practice.

One looks with both eyes at the tip of the nose, sits upright
and in a comfortable position, and holds the heart to the center in the midst of conditions. In Taoism it is called the yellow
middle, in Buddhism the center in the midst of conditions. The
two are the same. It does not necessarily mean the middle
of the head. It is only a matter of fixing one's thinking on the
point which lies exactly between the two eyes. Then all is
well. The light is something extremely mobile. When one fixes
the thought on the mid-point between the two eyes, the light
streams in of its own accord. It is not necessary to direct the
attention especially to the central castle. In these few words
the most important thing is contained.

The center in the midst of conditions is a very subtle expression. The center is omnipresent; everything is contained
in it; it is connected with the release of the whole process of
creation. The condition is the portal. The condition, that is, the
fulfillment of this condition, makes the beginning, but it does
not bring about the rest with inevitable necessity. The meaning
of these two words is very fluid and subtle.

Without a doubt, the concept of a "center" in the midst of conditions—conditions such as being a person in a busy world—is one of the most powerful concepts conveyed by the Old Master. It also was key to my success with this method. Today, after 50 years have passed, I still use this concept to get myself in the right mindset for deep meditation. As the Master said: "The condition is the portal." When an idle moment occurs in the busyness of personality and worldly activity, all I have to think is, "the center in the midst of conditions," and I'm shifting into meditation's blessed rest and renewal. And when in meditation with my mind full with the world's business, I simply bring forth the mantra, "the center in the midst of conditions," and I'm centered. I'm centered because I have come know how deeply content and sublimely happy I am when in that centeredness.

However, as I said before we started reading this Taoist text, the conditions of incarnate life are purposeful and intentional. Our souls sought this incarnation and have a destiny with the people and circumstances in this life. The conditions are important and should get our attention with the purpose of making relationships and situations better because we were here and engaged them mindfully. What makes this soul mission succeed is budgeting time to enter into the center in the midst of these conditions. Centering with the Light brings out our better selves and draws the Infinite Eternal into our relationships and circumstances. The goal is for the finite and infinite to work together and thereby unite again. The inner and the outer, the universal and the individual reunite rather than remain separated. This union (the literal meaning of the Sanskrit word, *yoga*) is the ideal.

Fixating contemplation is indispensable; it ensures the making fast of the enlightenment. Only one must not stay sitting rigidly if worldly thoughts come up, but one must examine where the thought is, where it began, and where it fades out. Nothing is gained by pushing reflection further. One must be content to see where the thought arose, and not seek beyond the point of origin; for to find the heart, that cannot be done.

Here the Old Master is teaching us that one cannot get beyond consciousness with consciousness. One cannot get beyond thinking by thinking. We must be content to see where the thoughts arise from, and seek to get beyond that origin. When worldly thoughts arise, and they will, one needs to notice what started them, and having identified their cause, subdue that influence. I often put a pad of paper and a pen next to me when meditating; then, when important *worldly* thoughts come, I stop and write them on the pad. This *removes* their distractive power. My lower mind knows that I have written them down and will attend to them later. Eventually, I have settled my busy worldly mind and assured it that I am aware of the worldly things that need attention. In this way my worldly mind gets quiet. Then, I can move on with the higher dimensions of the centered oneness in deep stillness.

> Together we want to bring the states of the heart to rest, that is true contemplation. What contradicts it is false contemplation. That leads to no goal. When the flight of the thoughts keeps extending further, one should stop and begin contemplating. Let one contemplate and then start fixating again. That is the double method of making fast the enlightenment. It means the circulation of the light. The circulation is fixation. The light is contemplation. Fixation without contemplation is circulation without light. Contemplation without fixation is light without circulation! Take note of that!

Here again the Old Master gives a magic way to unlock the door to higher perception and enlightenment. If my mind is just too busy, too anxious, too upset, too blue or too excited, I stop. I get up, stretch and rearrange things, then sit back down and try again. Fighting distractions leads nowhere. Getting angry with oneself leads nowhere. Another danger is false attunement. I can always tell when my reflection was not true because I "wake" feeling no contentment. Much of our trouble with this teaching can be found in our definition of "contemplation." To us it is deep thought or focused thought. But we just learned that we cannot get beyond thinking by thinking! Thought is not what is meant by this type of contemplation. What we seek is *mindful awareness* without thought. It is a state of full mental *awareness and* perfect stillness. The essence of consciousness without movement or conception. When the master uses the term "fixation," it is *centering!* All of our bodily energies and mental stirrings are always "doing their thing."

By taking hold of them and circulating them we gain control and the circulation eventually centers consciousness in stillness and magic emptiness. Now, we must add the Light. The Light comes as from out of nowhere when there is awareness in quiet emptiness. When this happens, we have the master's teaching in hand.

4. Circulation of the Light and Making the Breathing Rhythmical

Leave the Increase to Natural Forces
The Heart and the Breath

Here the Old Master directs us not to attempt to dictate how it should all happen and what the result should be. Rather, leave these to the universal forces that have a natural flow toward the ideal, the perfected, and ultimate oneness. However, this is not a direction toward doing little to nothing, no. We must devote our whole being to *the process*. It simply means that we trust in the process and the natural flow toward the ideal outcome. Frankly, we can't even imagine "the peace that passes understanding" that is ours to know.[87] Do our part faithfully, and the benefits will flow to us.

> The Old Master said, The decision must be carried out with a collected heart, and not seeking success; success will then come of itself: In the first period of release there are chiefly two mistakes: indolence and distraction. But that can be remedied; the heart must not enter into the breathing too completely. Breathing comes from the heart. What comes out of the heart

is breath. As soon as the heart stirs, there develops breath-energy. Breath-energy is originally transformed activity of the heart. When our ideas go very fast they imperceptibly pass into fantasies which are always accompanied by the drawing of a breath, because this inner and outer breathing hangs together like tone and echo. Daily we draw innumerable breaths and have an equal number of fantasies. And thus, the clarity of the spirit ebbs away as wood dries out and ashes die.

Around this whole planet in all ancient schools of enlightenment the importance of breath was taught for generations. In the biblical Genesis it is clearly stated that breath is life.[88] Here the Old Master is teaching that the breath and the heart are connected. I appreciate the line: "...this inner and outer breathing hangs together like tone and echo." The tone is our individual, finite effort and the echo is the universal, infinite response. As we apply ourselves, we receive. It is a natural, universal law.

So, then, should a man have no imaginings in his mind? One cannot be without imaginings. Should one not breathe? One cannot do without breathing. The best way is to make a medicine of the illness. Since heart and breath are mutually dependent, the circulation of the light must be united with the rhythm of breathing. For this, light of the ear is above all necessary. There is a light of the eye and a light of the ear. The light of the eye is the united light of the sun and moon outside. The light of the ear is the united seed of sun and moon within. The seed is thus the light in crystallized form. Both have the same origin and are different only in name. Therefore, understanding (ear) and clarity (eye) are one and the same effective light.

The Old Master is conveying teachings from the *Yinfu Jing* ("Book of Secret Correspondence"), also known as *Huangdi Yinfu Jing* ("Yellow Emperor's Book of Secret Correspondence"). For more on this see endnote 69.

This is a curious teaching. Mental images are apparently okay and, of course, breathing is okay (no surprise there). The Old Master takes what could be distractions and makes a vaccine of them—in other words, a little of the poison builds immunities to the more dangerous infection. Edgar Cayce joins the master in this by explaining that a three-dimensional mind cannot reach higher dimensions of consciousness without using its "imaginative forces."[89] He encourages us to use our imaginative forces to expand beyond our finite awareness and physical form. We need to reach up and out to a greater reality, an infinite, eternal reality—from the seen to the unseen. For example, the stars, planets, and galaxies that can be detected make up only 4 percent of the universe! *Four percent!* The other 96 percent is made up of essences that cannot be seen or easily explained. These invisible influences are called "dark energy" and "dark matter." Astronomers discovered their existence by noticing the gravitational influence that they exert on normal matter (the visible parts of the universe). Consider this further; the universe may contain as many as 100 *billion* galaxies, and each of these galaxies has within them *billions* of stars, massive clouds of gas and dust, countless planets and moons, and enormous amounts of cosmic debris—yet all of this is only 4 percent of the total mass and energy in the universe. We are living in a very small portion of reality. For us to move from our limited perception, we need to move from that which is seen to that which is unseen—to the influences beyond physicality.

The only element in our present being that can shift its finite condition is our *mind!* Mind is the bridge to infinity. And the first-stage rocket to get us beyond Earth's gravity is our *imagination.* We have to imagine rising and expanding out of this reality. The next-stage rocket is imagining the nature of infinity—something Cayce states is *innately* within us. Here's Cayce on this topic:

"The entity knows innately the RELATIONSHIP of the soul—or the first cause of self—with infinity; the relationship of infinity to each entity; and that there is no respecter of persons except as to how and why each entity, as a spark of infinity, magnifies or uses its relationship NOT for self-indulgence or gratification but for the GLORY of that which is the source of light, of all that pertains to light. For every spark of light, whether in the spiritual, the mental or the material sense, must have its inception in infinity."[90]

The Old Master's "eye" and "ear" metaphor is a fascinating one. I disagree with Wilhelm's insertion identifying ear with understanding and eye with clarity, but I understand what he was going for. I believe the Old Master was using the carnal eye as a condition that always looks *outward* toward this reality, but the Kingdom of God is *within* us.[91] Old Master uses "ear" as a symbol of *inner* perception and "eye" as a symbol of outer perception.

> In sitting down, after lowering the lids, one uses the eyes to establish a plumb-line and then shifts the light downward. But if the transposition downward is not successful, then the heart is directed towards listening to the breathing. One should not be able to hear with the ear the outgoing and intaking of the breath. What one hears is that it has no tone. As soon as it has tone, the breathing is rough and superficial, and does not penetrate into the open. Then the heart must be made quite light and insignificant. The more it is released, the less it becomes; the less it is, the quieter. All at once it becomes so quiet that it stops. Then the true breathing is manifested and the form of the heart comes to consciousness.

This passage is so important to our understanding and progress with the Master's method that I want to share Cleary's translation:

> When you sit, lower your eyelids and then establish a point of reference. Now let go. But if you let go absolutely, you may not be able to simultaneously keep your mind on listening to your breathing. You should not allow your breathing to actually be audible; just listen to its soundlessness. Once there is sound, you are buoyed by the coarse and do not enter the fine. Then be patient and lighten up a little. The more you let go, the greater the subtlety; and the greater the subtlety, the deeper the quietude. Eventually, after a long time, all of a sudden even the subtle will be interrupted and the true breathing will appear, whereupon the substance of mind will become perceptible.

Lowering our eyelids *automatically* shifts our consciousness. Research has found that shutting down sight *automatically* changes our brainwave patterns from beta to alpha and increases production of serotonin (a chemical messenger which transmits signals among brain cells and affects mood). Once this shift has occurred, we are to let go but not completely, for we have to maintain awareness of how we are breathing, quietly or audibly. If audibly, then we are still too much in the physical body. If quietly, then we are moving through dimensions of consciousness, and the "form of the heart" and the "substance of mind" will become perceptible.

> If the heart is light, [then] the breathing is light, for every movement of the heart affects breath-energy. If breathing is light, the heart is light, for every movement of breath-energy affects the heart. In order to steady the heart, one begins by taking care of the breath-energy. The heart cannot be influenced directly. Therefore, the breath-energy is used as a handle, and this is what is called maintenance of the concentrated breath-energy.

Our breath and breathing are controlled by our deeper nervous system, the autonomic. If we are attempting to control it using our outer nervous system, the cerebrospinal, then we are still in bodily consciousness, and that is not going to take us anywhere. However, shifting to conscious awareness of the autonomic breathing pattern also needs to change to a more subtle, shallow breathing. At first our breath may be deep and strong but gradually as we continue, we will hardly be breathing for the body is very still and quiet. This is when the deep consciousness is freed and a new perception arises. This is when the life-energy or breath-energy are ideal for the heart light to shine.

It is difficult to explain essence using substance, to explain inner realities using outer words, but in these passages the Old Master manages to teach what cannot be easily conveyed. I will attempt to expand on his skillful training: When we can bring vision into the stillness of looking but not seeing, then the heart is directed inward and may "listen" to the breathing. That is not to say that proper breathing is audible, it is not. This type of listening is more akin to *feeling and perceiving* than audibly hearing. The first step in quieting the heart is to understand that we are not talking about the human organ but more about human desire, caring, and longing. This is the heart that needs to be quiet. And the key to quietness is removing the distractions of desire, caring, and long‐ing. When the power of these is subdued, then the heart quiets down. When the heart is quiet, so is the breathing. The reverse is true as well; when the breathing is quiet, so is the heart. These two work together in bringing about the ideal condition for deep meditation. I loved the Old Master's description (see p. 24): "the heart with the wings of the lungs." That made them one for me in an angelic image.

Children, do you not understand the nature of movement? Movement can be produced by outside means. It is only an‐other name for mastery. One can make the heart move merely by running. Should one not also be able to bring it to rest by concentrated quietness? The great holy ones who knew how the heart and breath-energy mutually influence one another have thought out an easier procedure in order to help poster‐ity. In the *Book of the Elixir*[92] it is said: 'The hen can hatch her eggs because her heart is always listening.' That is an impor‐tant magic spell. The hen can hatch the eggs because of the energy of heat. But the energy of the heat can only warm the shells; it cannot penetrate into the interior. Therefore, she con‐ducts this energy inward with her heart. This she does with her hearing. In this way she concentrates her whole heart. When the heart penetrates, the energy penetrates, and the chick receives the energy of the heat and begins to live. Therefore, a hen, even when at times she leaves her eggs, always has the attitude of listening with bent ear. Thus, the concentration of the spirit is not interrupted. Because the concentration of the spirit suffers no interruption, neither does the energy of heat suffer interruption day or night, and the spirit awakens to life. The awakening of the spirit is accomplished because the heart has first died. When a man can let his heart die, then the primal spirit wakes to life. To kill the heart does not mean to let it dry and wither away, but it means that it has become undivided and gathered into one.

The Buddha said: 'When you fix your heart on one point,

then nothing is impossible for you.' The heart easily runs away, so it is necessary to concentrate it by means of breath-energy. Breath-energy easily becomes rough, therefore it has to be refined by the heart. When that is done, can it then happen that it is not fixed?

Here the Old Master uses a story, a parable to convey an important principle. This is one of my favorite enlightenment stories. He teaches that a hen hatches her eggs not by warmth alone but by listening with her centered heart. The master refers to this as a magic spell that we must use. Bodily heat is life, but it does not penetrate the depths of being or spark into existence the life–force. That is done through *penetrating* with the heart. And here again the master brings in the role of "hearing"; that is, the type of hearing that is akin to *feeling*. The master explains that even when outer life and relationships take us far from our meditation cushion, we can maintain an *unbroken connection* by carrying an attitude of ever–listening–for or caringly feeling the embryo of our spirit body. And because the concentration of the spirit connection is unbroken, life–energy magically transforms from potential energy to kinetic energy, from latent to manifest.

When the master states that this is all accomplished because "the heart has first died," he is referring to the selfish, self–seeking, self–gratifying lower nature and its heart full of desire, caring, and longing. "When a man can let his heart die, then the primordial spirit wakes to life." Cayce taught this amazing lesson with these words: Crucify desire in self. Here is the whole teaching and more:

"Crucify desire in self; that you may be awakened to the real abilities of helpfulness that lie within your grasp." And he explains: "Without preparation, desires of EVERY nature may become so accentuated as to destroy . . ."[93] Crucifying or dying to the longings, cares, and desires of our lower, self–centered nature makes possible the enlightenment and renewal of our spiritual, eternal nature! Cayce adds: " . . . death in the physical is the birth in the spiritual, see?"[94]

Now, since we humans have such a tendency toward the swing to extremes, the Old Master added: "To kill the heart does *not* mean to let it dry and wither away, but it means that it is undivided and gathered into one." So often we approach spiritualization by withering away from sensuous life for fear of its negative effect on our soul growth. But, like young Siddhartha, we eventually come to know that this is fear-based, unhealthy, and not holistic. Like the great Buddha, we eventually discover that the *middle path* is the better way, and we grow spiritually by *integrating all aspects* in proper order and higher purposes. A true seeker is dynamically alive and filled with the essence of life. A true master knows all aspects of human life, and has mastery over those that weigh down a body, mind, and soul with heavy earthiness, loss of self-esteem, confusion, doubts, and despair. A true master has seen the demons within, and has shined the light upon them so as to reveal that they all wear masks, having little power, other than that which we give them. He and she know the triggers that awaken them. A true master walks between the dark and light, centered in the strength of his will made one with the will and way of Infinite Eternal One.

> The two mistakes of indolence and distraction must be combated by quiet work that is carried on daily without interruption; then success will certainly be achieved. If one is not seated in meditation, one will often be distracted without noticing it. To become conscious of the distraction is the mechanism by which to do away with distraction. Indolence of which a man is conscious, and indolence of which he is unconscious, are a thousand miles apart. Unconscious indolence is real indolence; conscious indolence is not complete indolence, because there is still some clarity in it. Distraction comes from letting the mind wander about; indolence comes from the mind's not yet being pure.

This teaching reminds me of Jesus's teaching about how we may think we are in the light when we are actually in darkness: "Your eye is the lamp of your body; when your eye is sound, your whole body is full of light; but when it is not sound, your body is full of darkness. Therefore, be careful lest the light in you be darkness. If then your whole body is full of light, having no part dark, it will be wholly bright, as when a lamp with its rays gives you light."[95] This always disturbed me on my journey, for it implied that we can actually fool ourselves into thinking we are in the light when actually we are in darkness. This forced me to be much more mindful of my true intentions, motivations, and the fruits of whatever I was thinking and doing. As the Old Master taught: "Indolence of which a man is conscious, and indolence of which he is unconscious, are a thousand miles apart." Maintaining a mindfulness about the light and dark nature of my vibrations and thoughts became very important to me, even if it was motivated by a little fear of deluding myself.

In this next lesson Wilhelm uses anima and animus again as darkness and light, so I have changed this to lower nature and higher nature.

> Distraction is much easier to correct than indolence. It is as in sickness: if one feels pains and irritations, one can help them with remedies, but indolence is like a disease that is attended by lack of realization. Distraction can be counteracted, confusion can be straightened out, but indolence and lethargy are heavy and dark. Distraction and confusion at least have a place, but in indolence and lethargy the lower nature alone is active. In distraction the higher nature is still present, but in indolence pure darkness rules. If one becomes sleepy during meditation, that is an effect of indolence. Only breathing serves to overcome indolence. Although the breath that flows in and out through the nose is not the true breath, the flowing in and out of the true breath takes place in connection with it.

Cleary translated this passage using the word "oblivion" rather than "indolence and lethargy," and "lower nature" rather than "anima." Curiously, in my own practice, I prefer the word "laziness," but I also prefer Cleary's words "lower nature" over "anima." Here is a sample of Cleary's translation:

> Oblivion means the lower nature is in complete control, whereas the lower nature is a lingering presence in distraction. Oblivion is ruled by pure darkness and negativity.

Cleary's translation using "oblivion" versus "indolence" is likely referring to the stupor–like state of insensibility, or that dazed state that we can get into when not mindfully present. Here the old Master is talking about a state of consciousness that is like a fog in a mind that is uncentered and not consciously alert.

I've experienced this state during practice sessions. I've also become conscious of being in a daze during the practice. For me, the word laziness better fits both the cause and condition of this state. "Lower nature" better fits the portion of my being that is involved, rather than the term "anima." This is because I feel "anima" to be a *complementary* portion of my whole being, not the dark side of my being, and especially not the evil or negative side. As the master stated, only reengaging the circulation breath can bring us out of the daze, for it captures the mind again.

Edgar Cayce's input is helpful here, because he saw our soul as a much larger portion of our being than we my think it is. He also taught that our soul has levels to its *states* of consciousness. A lower level is in our body and associated with sleep and dreaminess. However, Cayce stated that sleepiness was not a sign of our weakness during meditating but a *normal early phase* in one's spiritual practice. As any beginner gets nearer the deeper self, he or she is moving into the same condition that leads to sleep: quiet body, the mind clear of daily busyness, and slipping into the subconscious, dreaming portion of our being—thus, resulting in sleep. Cayce taught that as one's practice continued, this tendency toward sleepiness would gradually fade. The meditator would become semi–conscious of being almost asleep. As the meditator continued diligently, he or she would become *fully* conscious of being in a sleep–like state, which is not actual sleep but mindfulness while in one of the deeper states of consciousness.[96]

Unconscious to semi–conscious awareness of being spacy is not a desirable place to be, and it will not yield positive benefits. One must recapture mindfulness and center it on the goal of the practice, and this while being in a condition *similar* to sleep. The Old Master's method of breaking out of the daze is to use the circulation of the breath, and in this case he is speaking of the *physical* breath—later the spiritual "breath" will circulate as well. The breakthrough is achieved using the physical breath which then awakens the spiritual breath.

In this next passage the Old Master repeats the teaching:

While sitting, one must therefore always keep the heart quiet and the energy concentrated. How can the heart be made quiet? By the breath. Only the heart must be conscious of the flowing in and out of the breath; it must not be heard with the ears. If it is not heard, then the breathing is light; if light, it is pure. If it can be heard, then the breath-energy is rough; if rough, then it is troubled; if it is troubled, then indolence and lethargy develop and one wants to sleep. That is self-evident.

How to use the heart correctly during breathing must be understood. It is a use without use. [Try to *feel* or *intuit* the deeper meaning in this paradoxical statement, "It is a use without use."] One should only let the light fall quite gently on the hearing. This sentence contains a secret meaning. What does it mean to let the light fall? It is the spontaneous radiation of the light of the eyes. The eye looks inward only and not outward. To sense brightness without looking outward means to look inward; it has nothing to do with an actual looking within. What does hearing mean? It is the spontaneous hearing of the light of the ear. The ear listens inwardly only and does not listen to what is outside. To sense brightness without listening to what is outside is to listen inwardly; it has nothing to do with actually listening to what is within. In this sort of hearing, one hears only that there is no sound; in this kind of seeing, one sees only that no shape is there. If the eye is not looking outward and the ear is not hearkening outward, they close themselves and are inclined to sink inward. Only when one looks and hearkens inward does the organ not go outward nor sink inward. In this way indolence and lethargy are done away with. That is the union of the seed and the light of the sun and moon.

If, as a result of indolence, one becomes sleepy, one should stand up and walk about. When the mind has become clear one should sit down again. If there is time in the morning, one may sit during the burning of an incense stick, that is the best. In the afternoon, human affairs interfere and one can therefore easily fall into indolence. It is not necessary, however, to have an incense stick. But one must lay aside all entanglements and sit quite still for a time. In the course of time there will be success without one's becoming indolent and falling asleep.

When we are honest with ourselves, we know that the meditation has lost its way and we are in a stupor or daze. There is no reason to continue because we have indeed drifted out of the true path. It is best to stop meditating, get up and walk around, move the body, stretch, play some music, light incense, and the like. I highly recommend the music created by Karunesh, specifically "Ancient Voices" from the album *Call of the Mystic* and "Calling Wisdom" from the album *Zen Breakfast*, all available via amazon.com. Then, try the meditation again.

Early in my training and practice, the use of incense, mystical music, and candlelight were very helpful. I felt that since I don't use these in daily life activity, my subconscious reacted to my using them, and thereby accepted that this was meditation time. I also meditated in the same place and time each day, adding to my subconscious's sense of meditation time. My body and mind took these outer suggestions as signals, and began shifting into the meditative condition. It is just how Pavlov's dogs responded to the stimulus of a metronome to begin salivating because the sound meant that it was time to eat. After years of practice I no longer needed these items to suggest meditation. The transition was so familiar and easy that I could meditate anywhere, anytime—and I did so, on airplanes, in airports, hotel rooms, even while sitting in waiting rooms. I even got to where I could slip into a semi-meditative condition while listening to someone talking to me. In these cases, it gave me access to *intuition*, providing me with better understanding of the person and possibly an insight that might help the person. I did have to be aware of my visual and tonal prejudices, because the person could have features and tones that made me uncomfortable or distracted. Getting personal prejudices subdued was very difficult, sometimes near impossible. I think a cause for this came from past lives and habit patterns that generated a karmic condition in me that was difficult to change. Being *aware of my prejudices* helped me subdue them to a degree while in contact with someone else. It was as if I became two people, one affected by the person and the other observing their effect on me. I'm not just speaking about negative features and tones; beauty and pleasant tones were more often my prejudices, and would interfere with clear, true intuitive insights from my deeper consciousness that was in closer contact with the universal, collective consciousness. Edgar Cayce taught to us to "watch self," so that the purer awareness may come through us.[97]

5. Mistakes During the Circulation of the Light

Errors

The Old Master said: Your work will gradually become concentrated and mature, but before you reach the condition in which you sit like a withered tree before a cliff, there are still many possibilities of error which I would like to bring to your special attention. These conditions are recognized only when they have been personally experienced. I shall enumerate them here. My school differs from the Buddhist yoga school (*Chan-tsung*) [School of Meditation in medieval China] in that it has confirmatory signs for each step of the way. First I would like to speak of the mistakes and then of the confirmatory signs.

Cleary's translation of this opening teaching is worth reading:

Even though your practice gradually matures, "there are many pitfalls in front of the cliff of withered trees." This makes it necessary to elucidate the experiences involved in detail. Only when you have personally gotten this far do you know how I can talk of it now. Our school is not the same as Chan study in that we have step-by-step evidences of efficacy. Let us first talk about points of distinction, then about evidences of efficacy.

Now back to Wilhelm and Baynes's edition:

> When one begins to carry out one's decision, care must be taken so that everything can proceed in a comfortable, relaxed manner. Too much must not be demanded of the heart. One must be careful that, quite automatically, heart and energy are co-ordinated. Only then can a state of quietness be attained. During this quiet state the right conditions and the right space must be provided. One must not sit down (to meditate) in the midst of frivolous affairs. That is to say, the mind must be free of vain preoccupations. All entanglements must be put aside; one must be detached and independent. Nor must the thoughts be concentrated upon the right procedure. This danger arises if too much trouble is taken. I do not mean that no trouble is to be taken, but the correct way lies in keeping equal distance between being and not being. If one can attain purposelessness through purpose, then the thing has been grasped. Now one can let oneself go, detached and without confusion, in an independent way.
>
> Furthermore, one must not fall victim to the ensnaring world. The ensnaring world is where the five kinds of dark demons disport themselves.

There are many classifications of demons throughout human history, and most of them correlate to the deadly sins, and archetypes associated with these sins. I consider the "five kinds of dark demons" to be the tantalizing energies of the five senses of the human body combined with sensual fantasies in the lower mind (fame, power, gratification, sex, and materialism). These hold us in the heavy, fleshy dimensions of life, weighing us down and keeping us from ascending into the spiritual, ethereal dimensions. The fleshy dimensions are so substantial and present with us; but the spiritual dimensions are so airy and tenuous as to be shadowy and difficult to grasp. Again, it reminds me of Jesus's teaching that the spirit is like the wind.[98]

When I first began training and practicing, the Old Master's paradoxical statements actually helped me "feel" the reality he was trying so hard to convey to us: "between being and non-being," "purposelessness through purpose," and "inaction through action." At deeper levels within me I could "feel" these truths. Of course, *experiencing* them was another matter. Through attention to the method and regular practice, a bridge was built that connected being with non-being, purpose with purposelessness, and action with non-action. After much time and true devotion to the mission, I could live comfortably in the two realities. Ancient Egyptian mysticism helped, especially the teachings about the powers of Hermes Trismegistus (this was his Greek name— he was called Thoth in Egyptian, and Enoch in Hebrew). Hermes could live in the two worlds, as symbolized in his icon of the ibis bird, who lives on the shore—between the depths of the sea with its treasures hidden beneath its surface appearance—and the lands and mountains of this visible world. I understood this to be living between the inner subconscious dimensions and the outer conscious dimensions.

> This is the case, for example, when, after fixation, one has chiefly thoughts of dry wood and dead ashes, and few thoughts of the resplendent spring on the great earth. In this way one sinks into the world of darkness. The power is cold there, breathing is heavy, and many images of coldness and decay display themselves. If one tarries there long one enters the world of plants and stones.
>
> Nor must a man be led astray by the ten thousand ensnarements. This happens if, after the quiet state has begun, one after another all sorts of ties suddenly appear. [This is often referred to as the "associative process" where images and thoughts keep coming via an endlessly linked chain of images and ideas.] One wants to break through them and cannot; one follows them, and feels relieved by this. This means the master has become the servant. If a man tarries in this state long he enters the world of illusory desires.
>
> At best, one goes to Heaven; at the worst, one goes among

the fox-spirits. Such a fox-spirit might also occupy himself in the famous mountains enjoying the wind and the moon, the flowers and fruits, and taking his pleasure in coral trees and jeweled grass. [Fox–spirit is a mythical *shapeshifter* in Chinese mythology. It is the attention–getting imagery generated by the lower subconscious.] But after he has been occupied thus for three to five hundred years, or at the most, for a couple of thousand years, his reward is over and he is born again into the world of turmoil. [This refers to how our immortal soul's many incarnations generate an earthly focus that eventually provides *no spiritual nourishment.*]

All of these are wrong paths. When a man knows the wrong paths, he can then inquire into the confirmatory signs.

Cleary's translation is helpful here.

> Don't fall into the elements of body and mind, where material and psychological illusions take charge. If you tend to fall into a deadness whenever you go into meditation and are relatively lacking in growth and creative energy, this means you have fallen into a shadow world. Your mood is cold, your breath sinking, and you have a number of other chilling and withering experiences. If you continue this way for a long time, you will degenerate into a blockhead or a rock head. Once you have gone into quietude and all sorts of loose ends come to you for no apparent reason, you find you cannot turn them away if you want to, and you even feel comfortable going along with them. This is called the master becoming the servant. If this goes on long, you fall into the various roads of the realms of form and desire.

This world we have been born into has many realms of form and desire, both externally and within the first layers of our lower mind. We must learn to be mindful of these and learn how to move beyond them to higher realms of existence and perception. Yet, as I warned in the beginning, this outer world is purposeful and our soul intentionally chose to enter here or were karmically drawn here for an opportunity for soul growth and liberation from the wheel of karma.

6. Confirmatory Experiences During the Circulation of the Light

Evidence of Progress

The Old Master said: There are many kinds of confirmatory experiences. One must not content oneself with small demands but must rise to the thought that all living creatures have to be redeemed. One must not be trivial and irresponsible in heart, but must strive to make deeds prove one's words.

If, when there is quiet, the spirit has continuously and un-interruptedly a sense of great joy as if intoxicated or freshly bathed, it is a sign that the light-principle is harmonious in the whole body; then the Golden Flower begins to bud.

After a few years of practicing (throughout my 30s) I experienced this "gaiety" and "intoxication," often called "bliss." It was so exciting that it became the apex of my practice in those days—which was *not* the ultimate goal. Even so, I enjoyed this bliss so much that it would affect my attitude and behavior all day. My children could see that I had meditated well and would make positive comments about me. They could also discern when I had had a poor meditation or missed meditation.

But in these early days I was quite faithful to the practice.

> When, furthermore, all openings are quiet, and the silver moon stands in the middle of heaven, and one has the feeling that this great earth is a world of light and brightness, that is a sign that the body of the heart opens itself to clarity. It is a sign that the Golden Flower is opening.
>
> Furthermore, the whole body feels strong and firm so that it fears neither storm nor frost. Things by which other men are displeased, when I meet them, cannot becloud the brightness of the seed of the spirit. Yellow gold fills the house; the steps are of white jade. Rotten and stinking things on earth that come in contact with one breath of the true energy will immediately live again. Red blood becomes milk. The fragile body of the flesh is sheer gold and diamonds. That is a sign that the Golden Flower is crystallized.

In the midst of the many challenges during my 40s the inner strength and stability gained by this Golden Flower practice got me through. Each day my meditations brought me to a centered state of peace and contentment. Curiously, the bliss experiences that I knew in my 30s shifted to a life-stabilizing centeredness. It is that state that the Old Master has called, "the center in the midst of conditions." My highs were never too high and my lows were never too low. I was a centered man—most of the time. Of course, there are events and relationships that can knock one off track, but when the core of one's being is tuned to the Infinite Eternal Oneness, and reattunes to it regularly, recovery is swift. That is not to say that the wound is gone. The initial blow may be over, but the bruise or wound remains and needs healing. Such healing usually comes through a period of self-reflection while in the Light.

Here is more on this in the Old Master's next lesson:

> The *Book of Successful Contemplation* (*Ying-kuan-ching*) says: "The sun sinks in the great water and magic pictures of trees in rows arise." The setting of the sun means that in chaos (in the world before phenomena, that is before the intelligible

world) the foundation is laid: that is the non-polarized condition (*wu-chi*) [means something like *ultimateless*]. Highest good is like water, pure and spotless. It is the ruler of the great polarity, the god who appears in the trigram of shock, Chen. [In the *I Ching*, Chen represents thunder, spring, east, and wood.] Chen is also symbolized by wood, and so the image of trees in rows appears.

A sevenfold row of trees means the light of the seven body-openings (or heart-openings). The northwest is the direction of the Creative. When it moves on one place further, the Bottomless Depth is there. [Here Wilhelm used the word "Abysmal," not in the normal meaning of "very bad," but rather the rare meaning of being "deep" or "depths." Cleary translated this as "great body of water." I have changed Abysmal to *Bottomless Depth*.] The sun which sinks into the great water is the image for the Creative and the Bottomless Depth. The Bottomless Depth is the direction of midnight (mouse, *tzu*, north) [here *tzu* means the *noble* north, symbolized as the North Star, Polaris). At the winter solstice, thunder (*Chen*) is in the middle of the earth quite hidden and covered up. Only when the trigram Chen is reached does the light-pole appear over the earth again. That is the image represented by the rows of trees. The rest can be correspondingly inferred.

Here Wilhelm's translation uses "the trigram Chen" from the *I Ching*. But, Chen also refers to one of the "signs" in the Chinese zodiac, the *Chen Dragon*. The Chen Dragon is the fifth of the 12–year cycle of animals which appear in the Chinese zodiac. It is the only zodiac sign represented by a mythic creature, rather than a real animal. The influence of the Chen Dragon is power and vitality. I prefer translating this passage using the Chen Dragon's power and vitality that comes when "the light–pole appears over earth again"—possibly meaning the North (polar) Star over Earth as a heavenly guiding light.

Cleary's translation of this verse is quite different from Wilhelm's, having no references to "winter solstice thunder" or zodiac signs. Cleary wrote that the original text that Wilhelm purchased from an antique–

book shop in China was "a garbled translation of a truncated version of a corrupted recension of the original work." Even so, Cleary concedes, "the book made a powerful impression. It became one of the main sources of Western knowledge of Eastern spirituality and also one of the seminal influences in Jungian thought on the psychology of religion." As I have also stated, Wilhelm's text has been a seminal influence in my meditative life. That is why I am using it in this book, but adding Cleary's translation where appropriate and meaningful.

Now we go back to the Old Master's teachings. The following paragraph is virtually the same in Wilhelm's *and* Cleary's translations.

> The second part [or stage] means the building of the foundation on this. The great world is like ice, a glassy jewel-world. The brilliancy of the light gradually crystallizes. Hence a great terrace arises and upon it, in the course of time, the Buddha appears. When the golden being appears who should it be but the Buddha? For the Buddha is the golden holy man of the great enlightenment. This is a great confirmatory experience.

We need to understand that the community of heavenly souls that descended into the third dimension of life, the physical realm, gradually lost their awareness of the spiritual, ethereal dimensions—which were their original realms and to which they are destined to return. Therefore, throughout the ages of this community's incarnations there appeared from time to time enlightened souls who spoke of higher realms of life and consciousness. Buddha, Siddhartha Gautama, was one of these. In the Bible of the Western world this worldwide community of souls is called the "Morning Stars" in chapter 38:7 of the book of Job. In this same chapter God questioned Job after Job's successful victory over Satan's many tests. One of the questions in verse 38:4 was, "where were you when I (God) set the foundations of the Earth?" According to Cayce, the foundations of the earth were laid long before Job's physical incarnation, so the question has many implications about Job's greater nature being an immortal soul. Job and our souls were born as spiritual beings long before the earth was created. We are now only temporarily incarnating as physical beings. Unfortunately, the world and the wheel of incarnations have come to possess us, holding us in physicality and self-consciousness. These have created many materialistic desires and habits that capture our attention. Buddha was a light to humanity, teaching about liberation from these possessive desires and habit patterns that bind us to this world.

The Old Master is acknowledging Buddha's enlightenment and telling us that we will come to that very same awareness as our meditative practice develops. He is telling us that this is one of the *confirmations* that we are making progress. In my experiences with this practice these moments come occasionally and fleetingly, but when they have come they affected me profoundly. They also gave me encouragement to keep on. After a few years of practice the moments of Buddha-like enlightenment came more frequently and remained for longer periods. Eventually, they became familiar and natural to my consciousness.

In the next passage the Old Master uses two descriptive phrases: "the gods are in the valley" and "the presence of the gods in the valley." From my years of studying ancient teachings and visiting ancient sites, seeing their imagery and translating their inscriptions, I have come to believe that human mythology contains the concept of "gods" because we were once and continue to be "godlings" of the Great God. As I wrote earlier, "godlings" is a term used by the ancient Egyptians, who also taught that we are rays of the Ra or Ray (Ra was originally pronounced *ray*). Originally, we were *celestial* beings who pushed our way into matter. We became possessed by the form-world, the amazing sensations of the physical body, and the excitement of *individualness*. This push resulted in our losing awareness of our celestial nature and the vast spiritual realms that we once roamed freely as a soul group. Edgar Cayce spoke of how all of us are the "little I am" spirits inside of the "Great I AM" Spirit. He explained that there are many dimensions to life and that our souls experience these many realms in our journey to full consciousness. Here's one example from his files:

"As an entity passes on from this present time or THIS solar system, THIS sun, THESE forces, it passes through the various spheres—leading first into that central force known as Arcturus—nearer the Pleiades on and on through the EONS of time or space. [Cayce identified the star Arcturus as the stargate in and out of our present system.[99]] Eventually, an entity passes into the inner forces, INNER sense, then they may again—after a period of nearly ten THOUSAND years—enter into the earth to make manifest those forces gained in ITS passage. In entering, the entity takes on those forms that may be known in the dimensions of that plane which it occupies, there being not only three dimensions as of the earth—but there may be seven as in Mercury, or four in Venus, or five in Jupiter. There may be only one as in Mars. There may be many more as in those of Neptune, or they may become even as nil—until purified in Saturn's fires."[100]

Edgar Cayce also spoke about the "openness" that the Old Master identified as "an echo in a valley." Cayce said that this results from our rising out of individual, finite consciousness into universal, infinite consciousness. He warned that we must shield ourselves, surround ourselves (body and mind) with the protection found in the *highest ideal* that we can conceive or imagine. Of course, for the mystical Christian that Cayce was, this protection was the "Christ Consciousness" and the "Christ Spirit." In one of his readings he explained that Christ Consciousness is "God Consciousness."[101] Jesus spoke to this too, telling how he did nothing and taught nothing that he had not received or been shown from our Heavenly Father. Jesus was tuned to and listening to the Divine Father/Mother in consciousness. Cayce wanted each meditator to surround their body and thoughts with the awareness, energy, and protection of the *creative* forces and vibrations, as opposed to the negative, destructive forces.[102] For Cayce the destructive forces were both *within* us and *around* us. In my years of practice I found a protective prayer and mental shield to be most helpful—that is, with my own demons and with those that seek to deceive and possess any channel of light and goodness.

Let's return to the Old Master's teaching:

> Now, there are three confirmatory experiences which can be tested. The first is that, when one has entered the state of meditation, the gods are in the valley. Men are heard talking as though at a distance of several hundred paces, each one quite clear. But the sounds are all like an echo in a valley. One can always hear them, but never oneself. This is called the presence of the gods in the valley.
>
> At times the following can be experienced: as soon as

one is quiet, the light of the eyes begins to blaze up, so that everything before one becomes quite bright as if one were in a cloud. If one opens one's eyes and seeks the body, it is not to be found any more. This is called: "In the empty chamber it grows light." Inside and outside, everything is equally light. That is a very favorable sign.

Or, when one sits in meditation, the fleshly body becomes quite shining like silk or jade. It seems difficult to remain sitting; one feels as if drawn upward. This is called: "The spirit returns and touches heaven." In time, one can experience it in such a way that one really floats upward. [After much practice, I had this buoyant, floating upward feeling often. At times I felt like I was levitating, but I never wanted to stop the meditation to see if I really was.]

And now, it is already possible to have all three of these experiences. But not everything can be expressed. Different things appear to each person according to his disposition. If one experiences these things, it is a sign of a good aptitude. With these things it is just as it is when one drinks water. One can tell for oneself whether the water is warm or cold. In the same way a man must convince himself about these experiences, only then are they real. [As subtle as many of these experiences are, and they are very wispy, gossamer-like, one may indeed know them. The challenge is that the gross-self doubts any sensation that is not strong and opaque. The translucent, ultra-fine, delicate sensations are too easily missed, and sadly sometimes dismissed.]

After several years of practice, I actually felt my spirit return to and touch "heaven." For me, it felt like touching the *womb* of Mother God, or Creative Mother—a womb that my spirit had known well before the world was. Once touched, I was never the same again. My outer self could never fully dominate my consciousness again. In the Revelation the Apostle John spoke to this while experiencing his own, personal self-transcendence. He wrote that once we reach a certain level of enlightenment and experience a resurrection of our spirit, we do not experience the "second death" and we possess the "keys to death."[103]

Cayce taught that the second death is when those who have gained some degree of understanding fall away again into self-exaltation, accentuating the ego rather than the soul-self, and suffer the death of truth a second time.[104] This does not happen to those who have reunited with the true source of their being. They may not be able to articulate it, but they have been touched, and that never leaves them.

The Old Master also assures us that we will *naturally know* when what we are doing is correct, comparing this knowing to tasting water to determine if it is warm or cold. This knowing is *innately* ours.

7. The Living Manner of the Circulation of the Light

Don't Give Up, Correct Thoughts, Purify Reflexes

In this very short lesson, the Old Master encourages continuing on, keeping our thoughts properly managed, and understanding pure reflexes rather than *contrived* reflexes.

The Old Master said: When there is a gradual success in producing the circulation of the light, a man must not give up his ordinary occupation in doing it. [Occupation here refers to *situations* that arise in life rather than simply a job.] The ancients said, When occupations come to us, we must accept them; when things come to us, we must understand them from the ground up. If the occupations are properly handled by correct thoughts, the light is not scattered by outside things, but circulates according to its own law. Even the still invisible circulation of the light gets started this way; how much more, then, is it the case with the true circulation of the light which has already manifested itself clearly.

When in ordinary life one has the ability always to react

to things by reflexes only, without any admixture of a thought of others or of oneself, that is a circulation of the light arising out of circumstances. This is the first secret.

This idea of *neutral, unemotional,* and *dispassionate* reflexes, without any admixture of a thought of others or of oneself, is a condition in which the greater potential for *correct* responses may manifest. When we have the true Light circulating within us, our reflex is purer because the *Light* is influencing it. Now, don't take this to mean that we don't engage in any degree of discernment—we do—but not by using outer-world rules or ideas of what is proper. Rather, we *feel* the Light's reaction from within us, and allow its expression. Remember, if it is good and creative, then it produces goodness; if bad or destructive, then it results in harm. Jesus taught us to judge by the fruit it bears: "Are grapes gathered from thorns, or figs from thistles? So, every sound tree bears good fruit, but the bad tree bears evil fruit. A sound tree cannot bear evil fruit, nor can a bad tree bear good fruit."[105] Lessons like this one are difficult for human nature to comprehend and apply in life. It is the intuitive sense of the spirit of the law versus the letter of the law. When in the spirit, reflexes are spiritually motivated—they are pure and clear of earthiness and ego.

Cleary's translation is slightly different and adds some words:

If you manage affairs with accurate mindfulness, then the light is not overcome by things, so it will do to repeat this formless turning around of the light time and again. If you can look back again and again into the source of mind, whatever you are doing, not sticking to any image of person or self at all, then this is "turning the light around wherever you are." This is the finest practice. In the early morning, if you can clear all objects from your mind and sit quietly for one or two hours, that is best. Whenever you are engaged in work or dealing with people, just use this "looking back" technique, and there will be no interruption. If you practice in this way for two or three months, the realized ones in Heaven will surely come to attest to your experience.

Here again we see how we are known in Heaven, because the "realized ones" in Heaven are ascended fellow "godlings" and angels—and they *are aware of us.* In some cases, they actually help us and support us.

8. A Magic Spell for the Far Journey

A Magic Spell

This lesson opens with the Old Master teaching us a magic spell.

The Old Master said: Yü Ch'ing has left behind him a magic spell for the far journey:

> Four words crystallize the spirit in the space of energy. In the sixth month white snow is suddenly seen to fly. At the third watch the sun's disk sends out blinding rays. In the water blows the wind of the Gentle. Wandering in heaven, one eats the spirit-energy of the Receptive. And the still deeper secret of the secret: The land that is nowhere, that is the true home.

These verses are full of mystery. The meaning is: The most important things in the great Tao are the words: action through non-action. Non-action prevents a person from becoming entangled in form and image (materiality) [and self-centeredness]. Action in non-action prevents a person from sinking into numbing emptiness and dead nothingness. The effect depends entirely on the central One; the releasing of the effect is in the two eyes. The two eyes are like the pole of the Great Wain [This is a curious translation. The Great Wain is the group of stars that compose the Big Dipper, the "pole of the Great Wain" may be a reference to the pole star Polaris, but that is in the Little Dipper. The word "wain" usually means a *wagon*, but has the connotation "to move," which brings in Cleary again, who translated this as, "the great Way" while including the word "stars." Because of the precession of the equinoxes, the term "pole" may describe the small circle in the northern sky that *cycles* over a period of 25,772 years. The Wain then may simply be the region of the guiding pole star.] which turns the whole of creation; they cause the poles of light and darkness to circulate. The Elixir depends from beginning to end on one thing: the metal in the midst of the water, that is, the lead in the water-region. Heretofore we have spoken of the circulation of the light, indicating thereby the initial release which works from without upon what lies within. This is to aid one in obtaining the Master. It is for pupils in the beginning stages. They go through the two lower transitions in order to gain the upper one. After the sequence of events is clear and the nature of the release is known, heaven no longer withholds the Way, but reveals the ultimate truth. Disciples, keep it secret and redouble your effort!

All ancient temples and schools held secrets closely and carefully. Why keep secrets? Edgar Cayce taught that *spiritualization* must be the motivation, the intention of the heart of all enlightenment–seekers; otherwise, using the same methods we create a Frankenstein instead of a "godling" within the Infinite Eternal One![106] In the Asian world they taught that the Bird of Paradise has two wings; one wing is the right training and technique, the other wing is the *right heart*. The Bird of Paradise doesn't fly with only one wing; therefore, all disciples must be *tested* to determine where their heart is, to determine how true and pure their motivations are *before* the deeper secrets are given to them!

In this opening teaching the Old Master reveals that there are indeed stages and transitional phases to growth. We cannot jump into Heaven, we must *grow* to Heaven. Edgar Cayce agreed wholeheartedly.[107]

Next, the Old Master guides us to the center within and shows us how to develop and function from that place. This condition is calm, without highs and lows, operating from a detached state of contentment, yet affecting life for the good of all.

> The circulation of the light is the inclusive term. The further the work advances, the more does the Golden Flower bloom. But there is a still more marvelous kind of circulation. Till now we have worked from the outside on what is within; now we stay in the center and rule what is external. Hitherto it was a service in aid of the Master; now it is a dissemination of the commands of the Master. The whole relationship is now reversed. If one wants to penetrate the more subtle regions by this method, one must first see to it that body and heart are completely controlled, that one is quite free and at peace, letting go of all entanglements, untroubled by the slightest excitement, and with the heavenly heart exactly in the middle. Then let one lower the lids of the two eyes as if one received a holy edict, a summons to become the minister. Who would dare disobey? Then with both eyes one illumines the house of the Bottomless Depth (water, *K'an*) [Wilhelm/Baynes used the word "Abysmal" here; but they meant it in the sense of *deep* or *depth*. I have changed this to "Bottomless Depth," which better fits the original teacher's intention.] Wherever the Golden Flower goes, the true light of polarity comes forth to meet it. The Warm Affection (brightness, *Li*) [Here again I find Wilhelm/Baynes's translation of *Li* as "Clinging" not exactly the intention of the original teacher. However, I concede that the Chinese word "Li" is an abstract idea that may be translated in a number of different ways. I have replaced "Clinging" with "Warm Affection." The trigram Li has this connotation, also meaning *fire* and *brightness*.] is bright outside and dark within; this is the body of the Creative. The one dark

(line) enters and becomes master. The result is that the heart (consciousness) develops dependence on things, is directed outward, and is tossed about on the stream. When the rotating light shines towards what is within, it does not develop in dependence on things, the energy of the dark is fixed, and the Golden Flower shines concentratedly. This is then the collected light of polarity. Related things attract each other. Thus, the polarized light-line of the Bottomless Depth presses upward. It is not only the light in the deep, but it is creative light which meets creative light. As soon as these two substances meet each other, they unite inseparably, and there develops an unceasing life; it comes and goes, rises and falls of itself, in the house of the primal energy. One is aware of effulgence and infinity. The whole body feels light and would like to fly. This is the state of which it is said: Clouds fill the thousand mountains. Gradually it goes to and fro quite softly; it rises and falls imperceptibly. The pulse stands still and breathing stops. This is the moment of true creative union, the state of which it is said: The moon gathers up the ten thousand waters. In the midst of this darkness, the heavenly heart suddenly begins a movement. This is the return of the one light, the time when the child comes to life. [This is the rebirth or second birth of our original godly child–self—as Jesus attempted to teach Nicodemus.[108]]

However, the details of this must be carefully explained. When a person looks at something, listens to something, eyes and ears move and follow the things until they have passed. These movements are all underlings, and when the heavenly ruler follows them in their tasks it means: to live together with demons. [Remember that I consider the demons to be the tantalizing energies of the five senses combined with sensual fantasies in the lower mind (fame, power, gratification, sex, and materialism). These hold us in the heavy, fleshy dimensions of life, weighing us down and keeping us from ascending into the spiritual, ethereal dimensions.]

If now, during every movement and every moment of rest,

a person lives together with people and not with demons, then the heavenly ruler is the true man. When he moves, and we move with him, then the movement is the root of heaven. When he is quiet, and we are quiet with him, then this quietness is the cave of the moon. When he unceasingly alternates movement and rest, go on with him unceasingly in movement and quietness. When he rises and falls with inhaling and exhaling, rise and fall with him. That is what is called going to and fro between the root of heaven and the cave of the moon.

Notice how the Master reveals two natures within us, one is heavenly and the other is earthy. He teaches that one is the "root of heaven" and the other is the "cave of the moon." He teaches that the moon is stillness. The moon *reflects* the source of light, it does not generate light. The Master is teaching us that our present condition alternates between these two. Of course, the better way is to be active with people from the nonactive centered place from within heavenly consciousness.

Next, the Master teaches that willfully moving too soon or too late are weaknesses that must be mastered. We must become thus connected to and cooperating with the heavenly heart as it moves, not before or after it. And the key he gives us is the "house of the Creative"!

When the heavenly heart still preserves calm, movement before the right time is a fault of softness. When the heavenly heart has already moved, the movement that follows afterwards, in order to correspond with it, is a fault of rigidity. As soon as the heavenly heart is stirring, one must immediately mount upward whole-heartedly to the house of the Creative. Thus, the spirit-light sees the summit; this is the leader. This movement is in accord with the time. The heavenly heart rises to the summit of the Creative, where it expands in complete freedom. [The "Creative" is a repetitive concept that Cayce teaches, too.[109]] Then suddenly it demands the deepest silence, and one must lead it speedily and whole-heartedly into the yellow castle; thus, the eyes behold the central yellow dwelling place of the spirit.

When the desire for silence comes, not a single thought arises: he who is looking inward suddenly forgets that he is looking. At this time, body and heart must be left completely released. All entanglements have disappeared without trace. Then I no longer know at what place the house of my spirit and my crucible are. [The "crucible" is the body temple along with the mental temple of the mind. Spirit, in this context, would be the *essence* of our beingness.] If a man wants to make certain of his body, he cannot get at it. This condition is the penetration of heaven into earth, the time when all wonders return to their roots. So it is when the crystallized spirit goes into the space of energy. [This often causes me to think of Einstein's matter and energy. Energy can crystallize into matter and matter can return to energy. They are one, but may be expressed in different conditions.]

The One is the circulation of the light. When one begins, it is at first still scattered and one wants to collect it; the six senses are not active. This is the cultivation and nourishment of one's own origin, the filling up of the oil when one goes to receive life. [This passage is reminiscent of Jesus's teaching of the oil lamps of the 10 virgins ready to receive the heavenly bridegroom. Some had enough oil but some did not, so they missed the coming.[110]] When one is far enough to have gathered it, one feels light and free and need not take the least trouble. This is the quieting of the spirit in the space of the ancestors, the taking possession of former heaven. [Jesus refers to "former heaven" as that oneness he had with the Creator before the world was.[111]]

When one is so far advanced that every shadow and every echo has disappeared, so that one is entirely quiet and firm, this is refuge within the cave of energy, where all that is miraculous returns to its roots. One does not alter the place, but the place divides itself. This is incorporeal space where a thousand and ten thousand places are one place. One does not alter the time, but the time divides itself. This is immeasurable time when all the aeons are like a moment. [Cayce also taught this truth: "For, did the Father (or Infinity) bring the earth, the worlds into existence, how much greater is a day in the house of the Lord—or a moment in His presence—than a thousand years in carnal forces?" Cayce's parenthetical comment—"or Infinity"—equates "Father" with "Infinity."[112]]

As long as the heart has not attained absolute tranquillity, it cannot move itself. One moves the movement and forgets the movement; this is not movement in itself. Therefore, it is said: If, when stimulated by external things, one moves, it is the impulse of the being. If, when not stimulated by external things, one moves, it is the movement of heaven. [This is reminiscent of the Apostle John's comment in the Revelation: "I was in the Spirit on the Lord's day, and I heard behind me a great voice . . . and I *turned* to see the voice that spoke with me . . . "[113] I believe John was in deep meditation and he "turned" in consciousness, not physically. This is movement without outer stimulus, thus, "movement of heaven."] The being that is placed over against heaven can fall and come under the domination of the impulses. The impulses are based upon the fact that there are external things. They are thoughts that go on beyond one's own position. Then movement leads to movement. But when no idea arises, the right ideas come. [This is such a beautiful, insightful statement that it sends me to that place upon simply hearing it spoken.] That is the true idea. When things are quiet and one is quite firm, and the release of heaven suddenly moves, is this not a movement without purpose? Action through non-action has just this meaning.

As to the poem [the magic spell] at the beginning, the two first lines refer entirely to the activity of the Golden Flower. The two next lines are concerned with the mutual interpenetration of sun and moon. The sixth month is the Warm Affection. (Li, fire) [Wilhelm used the word "Clinging" here. The trigram is *Li*, has the quality of warmth and affection. I changed Clinging to Warm Affection.] The white snow that flies is the true polar darkness in the middle of the fire trigram [Li], that is about to turn into the Receptive. The third watch is the Bottomless Depth (*K'an*, water) [Wilhelm used the word *Abysmal*, I changed it to Bottomless Depth.] The sun's disk is the one polar line in the trigram for water [*K'an*, also means "to watch"], which is about to turn into the Creative. This contains the way to take the trigram for the Bottomless Depth [*K'an*, deep water] and the way to reverse the trigram for the Warm Affection (*Li*, fire) [*Li*, brightness and fire, with the connotation of warmth].

The following two lines have to do with the activity of the pole of the Great Wain [This is the group of stars that comprise the Big Dipper, thus the "pole" may be a reference to the small circle in the sky that is the region of the pole star. Because of the precession of the equinoxes, the position of the pole describes the small circle in the northern sky that cycles over a period of 25,772 years.], the rise and fall of the whole release of polarity. Water is the trigram of the Bottomless Depth; the eye is the wind of the Gentle (*Sun*). The light of the eyes illumines the house of the Bottomless Depth, and controls there the seed of the great light. 'In heaven', this means the house of the Creative (*Ch'ien*). "Wandering in heaven, one eats the spirit-energy of the Receptive." This shows how the spirit penetrates the energy, how heaven penetrates the earth; this happens so that the fire can be nourished.

Finally, the two last lines point to the deepest secret, which cannot be dispensed with, from the beginning to the end. This is the washing of the heart and the purification of the thoughts; this is the bath. [In Cayce's fascinating interpretation of the Revelation symbology he stated that the first 10 chapters were the purification of the body and its seven chakras, the next 10 chapters were the purification of the mind, and the last two chapters were the fulfillment of the promises.[114]] The holy science takes as a beginning the knowledge of where to stop, and as an end, stopping at the highest good. Its beginning is beyond polarity and it empties again beyond polarity.

The Buddha speaks of the transient, the creator of consciousness, as being the fundamental truth of religion. And the whole work of completing life and human nature in our Taoism lies in the expression 'to bring about emptiness.' All three religions agree in the one proposition, the finding of the spiritual Elixir in order to pass from death to life. In what does this spiritual Elixir consist? It means forever dwelling in purposelessness. [Here purposelessness is akin to *centered contentment*, but very much aware, though unmoved. It is observing with interpretation. It is affecting without attachment.] The deepest secret of the bath that is to be found in our teaching is thus confined to the work of making the heart empty. [Think of this empty heart as *quietly centered, still*.] Therewith the matter is settled. What I have revealed here in a word is the fruit of a decade of effort.

If you are not yet clear as to how far all three sections can be present in one section, I will make it clear to you through the threefold Buddhist contemplation of emptiness, delusion, and the center.

Emptiness comes as the first of the three contemplations. All things are looked upon as empty. Then follows delusion. Although it is known that they are empty, things are not destroyed, but one attends to one's affairs in the midst of the emptiness. But though one does not destroy things, neither does one pay attention to them; this is contemplation of the center. While practicing contemplation of the empty, one also knows that one cannot destroy the ten thousand things, and still one does not notice them. In this way the three contemplations fall together. But, after all, strength is in envisioning the empty. Therefore, when one practices contemplation of emptiness, emptiness is certainly empty, but delusion is empty too, and the center is empty. [It helps if we use our imaginative forces to intuit infinite, emptiness—the condition before the creation. In that emptiness was only consciousness, a universal consciousness perfectly still. There were no thoughts in this consciousness yet it was aware—but unmoved.] It needs a great strength to practice contemplation of delusion; then delusion is really delusion, but emptiness is also delusion, and the center is delusion too. Being on the way of the center, one also creates images of the emptiness; they are not called empty, but are called central. One practices also contemplation of delusion, but one does not call it delusion, one calls it central. As to what has to do with the center, more need not be said.

Note 1: Here Wilhelm writes a summary of the Chinese concepts. It is not part of the original Chinese text, so I don't include it. You can find this in his book. Included in his summary is a Wilhelm/Jung diagram that continues the idea that yin/feminine is dark, decays after death, is a ghost, not a god of the great God, and only the masculine yang leads to the fulfillment of the Golden Flower. I have created an alternative diagram using some of the terms and ideas that I will share in the next major section of the Chinese teachings. Using Pinyin, I am going to use *xing* in the place of Baynes's *hsing*, and that is going to give us a much improved view of yin and its partnership with yang.

Note 2: Cleary's translation ends here. He does not go on to the following book that Wilhelm included. However, as I mentioned earlier, I am working with Wilhelm's original book, so I am including this next book. I feel that it will add much to our study and understanding.

Book Two

The Book of Consciousness and Life

Translation of the
Hui Miung Ching

Written by Ch'an Buddist mink Liu Huayang in 1794

This classic Taoist text is a collection of eight poetically written stages along the way to expanding consciousness and living eternally. It includes signs and conditions that reveal success for each of the eight stages. Its primary teaching is the reunion of our whole being, the seen and the unseen.

These teachings and methods helped me find my original self through deep meditation, and then unite my outer life and personality with my inner, original self and its consciousness. Then, using Cayce and ancient Egyptian teachings, I learned to live cooperatively in both worlds, the outer and inner, the seen and unseen. Once the veil that separated these two parts of myself stopped being so subtle that I couldn't perceive it and so opaque that I couldn't see through it, progress flowed like a refreshing breeze. As Jesus taught, I began to have life "more abundantly.[115]"

Before I can go on, I have to explain how Chinese characters are westernized or romanized into our alphabet. There are two systems: Pinyin and Wade–Giles. I favor the Pinyin system because Pinyin was created by Chinese people for Chinese people and was officially adopted by the People's Republic of China in 1958. Whereas, Wade–Giles was created by two British scholars. To spare us too many distracting details I have put further information in the endnotes.[116] To our point in this study, Wade–Giles used *hsing*, as did Baynes in his translation of the

Golden Flower, but Pinyin used *xing*, both meaning the same thing.[117]

Remember how Baynes opened his translation of the Golden Flower using the English word "essence" for the Chinese word *hsing*. Then, he told us that from then on he was going to translate hsing as "human nature," if you remember— well, this decision is going to affect us now. Because I'm going to use xing in the place of Baynes's hsing. This is important because two keys to understanding this Taoist teaching are the terms *xing* (pronounced *shing*) and *ming*. These are truly difficult terms for English to clearly translate, and even in the many Taoist teachings there is inconsistency in defining these terms. I am fully aware of the challenges to my decision and the various parties who will view it with skepticism.

I've come to understand that xing means the *nature* of something, its *quintessential quality*. Ming came to mean the *expression, animation, or manifestation* of the essential nature, as well as its destiny and fate. Again, xing is the essential spark of existence while ming is the projected or animated *manifestation* of that spark. The projected portion operates under the universal law of karma—thus, its destiny and fate are affected by the use of free will. We may also think of ming as that which *contains* the essence. My soul–mind–body is the ming of my essence, my xing. These two terms have been described by Chen Yingning (a Taoist scholar from 1880–1969) as, "Xing and ming are like an oil lamp; ming is the oil and xing is the brilliance of the flame."[118] See my diagram on page 28 compared to Wilhelm/Jung's version, and notice how xing and ming complement one another. In my diagram yin contains xing, the unseen essence of the infinity dimensions, and yang contains ming, the seen projection of essence in the animated dimensions.

As a mystical Christian on this Taoist journey, my mind recalled that Jesus's essential nature appeared again in his resurrected body, and he did *physical* activities with his disciples and holy women while in the resurrected body—walking, talking, letting them touch him, and even eating fish and honey with them.[119] As I grew through these deep meditations, I came to see how my original essence (xing) may be expressed quite naturally through my projected self (ming), and the two may operate *cooperatively*, as Jesus did. Recall that he also entered back into the oneness of infinity with his resurrected body as a part of his whole being. He was no longer projected into this world. Notice also how his resurrected self was now one with his inner essence—revealing that there is nothing evil about the projected self. With this in mind, I first needed to unite these aspects of my whole being and practice cooperative living, mindful of both the infinite and the finite, both the universal and the individual, the unseen and the seen. At the same time, I had to be engaging with others in this temporarily projected incarnation for the purpose of resolving karma and sharing grace and love—as helpmeets one to another.

From here on I changed Wilhelm and Baynes's use of the term *human nature* to *inner essence*, because it better conveyed the Taoist teacher's intention (that is, in my opinion and experience). It could be translated as *consciousness*, as Baynes did, but we may confuse that with our everyday consciousness, which it is not. *Inner essence* better expresses the aspect of ourselves that we need to awaken, and then unite this with our animated life—*life* here meaning our condition of being expressed and animated. I've also changed the translation of ming from *life* to *animated life*—because it helps us better understand what we are talking about here.

1. Cessation of Outflowing

If thou wouldst complete the diamond body with no outflowing, Diligently heat the roots of inner essence and animated life. Kindle light in the blessed country ever close at hand, And there hidden, let your true self always dwell.

This is quite clear. To complete our new spirit body in the womb of our higher mind and heart, we need to awaken the *source* (roots). By now we surely understand that the *spirit* body's origin is not the sperm-and-egg of our *physical* mother and father. It is found in the transcendent, expansive dimensions of infinity. As I mentioned earlier, Edgar Cayce taught: "The entity knows innately—or the first cause of self—the *relationship* of the soul with infinity; the relationship of infinity to each entity."[120] His use of the word "innately" is what captured my attention when I first read this teaching; and the phrase "the first cause of self." This means that our connection to infinity is *inborn*; it is instinctive, intuitive. It is quite naturally who we are. It is *not* our *outer*, earthly, personality self. But we may grasp this innate knowing when we are near our *inner* selves, the part of us that dreams dreams and has moments of spontaneous insights, and awakens when in deep meditation. That part innately knows infinity and the first cause of self (the roots of existence).

How does this fit with the earlier teachings of the Old Master? It may seem a paradox to our present minds but inaction and non-being are xing, and action and being are ming. How can our essence be inaction and nonbeing? The answer has to be felt deep within, but I'll try to explain: Our essence is so completely one with infinity that it is impossible to distinguish it from the Infinite Eternal. Our essence is conscious within Infinite Consciousness. It is conscious but unmoved. It has never left its oneness with the Source of Life. On the other hand, our projected self has taken a journey through self-discovery and choice-making, interacting with others and situations. It is on a journey of growth and becoming, while our essence is the same yesterday, today, and tomorrow. Here are a few Bible passages that convey how our godly essence in God is unchanged:

"Lord, you have been our dwelling place for all generations. Before the mountains were brought forth, or ever you had formed the earth and the world, even from everlasting to everlasting, you are God." –Psalm 90:1–2 Notice how the infinite has been our dwelling place long before earth and the world existed.

"For I, the Lord, do not change." –Malachi 3:6

"Every good endowment and every perfect gift is from above, coming down from the Father of lights with whom there is no variation or shadow of change." –James 1:17 The light has always been on, it is we who have projected a portion of ourselves away from the light. But it is still there for us to return to.

"'I am the Alpha and the Omega,' says the Lord God, 'who is and who was and who is to come, the Almighty.'" –Revelation 1:8 We are a little "I am" inside the Great I AM, and this portion of us has never moved—the portion that did move as in the so-called beginning (Alpha), may return again along our journey (Omega).

Now let's continue with the wise monk's lesson:

> The subtlest secret of the Tao is inner essence and animated life. There is no better way of cultivating inner essence and animated life than to bring both back to unity. The holy men of ancient times [and many holy women], and the great sages, set forth their thoughts about the unification of inner essence and animated life by means of images from

the external world; they were reluctant to speak of it openly without allegories. Therefore, the secret of how to cultivate both simultaneously was lost on earth.

According to Cayce, this loss of wisdom *gradually* occurred as our souls projected themselves deeper and deeper into individualized self-consciousness and material bodies—losing awareness of the oneness to which we once were connected (and a portion is still connected). Cayce also explained that not only was this a movement into matter and physicality, it was a movement into *narrower* consciousness. Jung explained that a portion of our consciousness was *projected* outward into the physical-form world, forcing the depths of consciousness to *fall into our unconscious*.[121] There is a vast portion of our whole being that is behind a veil that separates our mind into three levels: personal conscious mind, soulful subconscious mind, and godly superconscious mind.

> What I show through a series of images is not a frivolous giving away of secrets. On the contrary, because I combined the notes of the *Leng Yen Ching* [see endnote 59] on the cessation of outflowing and the secret thoughts of *Hua Yen Ching*[122] with occasional references to the other sutras, in order to summarize them in this true picture, it can be understood that inner essence and animated life are not anything external to the germinal vesicle.

The choice of the word "vesicle" is revealing, for a vesicle is a small pouch or bladder enclosed by a membrane *within* a living organism, containing air or liquid. "Germinal" means the earliest stage of development. Wilhelm is using *germinal vesicle* as a metaphor for how *original* inner essence is *within* our present being, waiting to be awakened or born—more accurately: *re*awakened and *re*born. In ancient Egyptian art this is depicted as a *blue* portion of us (that is the *spiritual* portion) which is sealed in an enclosure waiting for the red-blood human portion to awaken it and free this sealed portion. See Egyptian illustration on page 115.

Now back to the teachings of this wise monk:

> I have drawn this picture [See illustration for Stage 2:
> Origin of the New Being in the Place of Power on p. 15]
> so that companions pursuing the divine workings of the dual
> cultivation may know that in this way the true seed matures,
> that in this way the cessation of outflowing is brought about,
> that in this way the *sheli* (*Sarira*, the human pearl, that is,
> the immortal body) is melted out, that in this way the great
> Tao is completed.
>   But the germinal vesicle is an invisible cavern; it has neither
> form nor image.

In this passage, the wise monk is breaking through our three–dimensional consciousness by undoing our mental construct of form and solidity. He is telling us that *this* vesicle has no form, no image. And it is not like a bladder but like a *cavern*—an *invisible* cavern. Interestingly, as physical and form–structured as we may have become, our minds are still capable of imagining a vast, invisible cavern of consciousness that is fertile, is capable of conception.

Another part of this lesson is "the dual cultivation" concept. As a mystical Christian I again see comparison between Taoist dual cultivation and Jesus's teaching. Remember when the scribe at the temple acknowledged the wisdom he overheard as Jesus was teaching others nearby? This caused the scribe to ask Jesus what was the most important commandment for spiritual seekers, and Jesus answered with more detail. Here's this conversation:

"One of the [temple] scribes came up and heard them disputing with one another, and seeing that he [Jesus] answered them well, asked him, 'Which commandment is the first of all?' Jesus answered, 'The first is: Hear, O Israel, The Lord our God, the Lord is one; and you shall love the Lord your God with all your heart, and with all your soul, and with all your mind, and with all your strength. The second is this: You shall love your neighbor as yourself. There is no other commandment greater than these.' And then the scribe said to him, 'You are right, Teacher; you have truly said that he is one, and there is no other but he; and to love him with all the heart, and with all the understanding, and with all the strength, and to love one's neighbor as oneself, is much more than all whole burnt offerings and sacrifices.' And when Jesus saw that the scribe answered wisely, he said to him, 'You are not far from the kingdom of God.'"[123]

I particularly appreciate how Jesus perceived the wisdom growing in this scribe and that he was close to full consciousness of the kingdom of God. The dual cultivation obviously means loving the Divine Infinite as well as the other souls that have projected from this Infinite One and with whom we share animated life—inner and outer cultivation.

The "outer self" is seeking to awaken the
"original self" using an offering.

The figure on the left is in the blood body, colored red, and the divine
figure on the right is in the spirit body, colored blue.

Notice that the spirit self is encased and separated from the outer self.
This scene is found on the walls of the tomb of Ramses III, KV 11.

In the following, the wise monk gives us the means to enliven the germinal vesicle—and that is the *vital breath* (prana).

When the vital breath stirs, the seed of this vesicle comes into being; when it ceases it disappears again. It is the place which harbors truth, the altar upon which inner essence and animated life are made. It is called the dragon castle at the bottom of the sea, the boundary region of the snow mountains, the primordial pass, the kingdom of greatest joy, the boundless country. All these different names mean this germinal vesicle. If a dying man does not know this germinal vesicle, he will not find the unity of inner essence and animated life in a thousand births, nor in ten thousand aeons. This germinal point is something great. Before this our body is born of our parents, at the time of conception, this seed is first created and inner essence and animated life dwell therein.

Edgar Cayce speaks to our lack of understanding about conception and gestation:

"It has been indicated, by the sage, the manner of growth in the womb is not understood by man; yet here you may find a concept of that development.

"That gland, a nucleus extending in the shape or form of a moving atom, gathers from its surroundings physical nourishment; and from the *mind* of the body it takes its PHYSICAL characteristics, or the *moulding* as it were of its features as related to the *external* expression.

"Then as the *mind* of the bearer binds those forces that are its natures in itself, its purposes, its desires, its hopes, its fears, these begin gradually to extend themselves through the nucleus; so that as the shape or form begins to find expression, there are also the channels through which the growth of the *spiritual being* gives its expression. [a morpho-genetic blueprint, *morphogenesis*]...

"In those glands that are eventually known as the geni-tal [first chakra], or in the lyden [second chakra], and the inner centers of thyroid [fifth chakra] through and from which the exterior forces are indicated in their activity,

there begins then the formation of the superficial circulation; that leads or connects between its *spiritual* import,
its *mental* purpose, and its *physical* development—for their
coordination. . .

"That is why in portions of the Scripture the extenuating
activities that take place in the *spiritual* being are described
by the expressions through those body centers."[124]

The Scripture that Cayce is referring to is found in The Revelation, where
Cayce explains that the Seven Churches of Asia Minor are outer symbols
of inner spiritual centers in the temple of the human body, and correlate
to the seven chakras.[125]

The symbols and scenes in this last book of the Bible represent experiences and stages through which we pass in our struggle to awaken again
spiritually and regain our close connection with God and the "Garden" that
we once shared. Cayce says that some symbols and places in Revelation
actually represent endocrine glands within our bodies and *thought patterns*
within our minds.[126] In his own words he explains: "The visions, the experiences, the names, the churches, the places, the dragons, the cities, all are but
emblems of those forces that may war within the individual in its journey
through the material, or from the entering into the material manifestation
[i.e., physical body and this world] to the entering into the glory, or the
awakening in the spirit . . . "[127]

As the Spirit moves through each church as a spiritual center within the
human body, it calls on the center to strengthen its virtues, overcome its
weaknesses, and to do what it knows to do, so that the final glory may be
achieved. This initial process is found in the first 10 chapters which help
prepare us for the spiritualization of our minds as described in the next
10 chapters of the Revelation. The last 2 chapters are the fulfillment of the
promises of resurrection and enlightenment.

Cayce explained that the Revelation was written for "those that were,
or will be, or may become," through their spiritual seeking, initiated into
an understanding of "the glories that may be theirs if they will but put
into work, into activity," the guidance and calling found in the text of the
vision. As the Spirit comes to each church and speaks to them, so Cayce
wants each of us to ask ourselves: "What is lacking in self? Are you cold?
Are you hot? Have you been negligent of the knowledge that is yours?

Are you stiff–necked? Are you adulterous in thought, in act, in the very glories that are yours?"[128]

Later in this book there is more on Cayce's symbolic interpretation of the Revelation.

Physicality is a shadow of spirituality, and the outer is a reflection of the inner—even to the point that physical conception and gestation reflects spiritual conception and gestation.

Back to the wise monk:

> The two are intermingled and form a unity, inseparably mixed like the sparks in the refining furnace, a combination of primordial harmony and divine law. Therefore, it is said: "In the state before the appearance there is an inexhaustible breath." Furthermore, it is said: "Before the parents have begotten the child, the breath of life is complete and the embryo perfect." But when the embryo moves and the embryo vesicle is torn, it is as if a man lost his footing on a high mountain: with a cry the man plunges down to earth, and from then on inner essence and animated life are divided. From this moment inner essence can no longer see animated life nor can animated life see inner essence. And now fate takes its course: youth passes over into maturity, maturity into old age, and old age into woe.

This is so true, and is the situation that we find ourselves in. We godlings of the Great God, rays from the Great Ray of Light, have slipped off a high mountain and plunged to earth. Our inner essence and animated life are now divided, and we can only burn the life forces so long when our projected body runs down and dies. And then the whole cycle begins again. We live in the river of karma, seeking and hoping for grace and resurrection to our original essence in spirit and expansive mindfulness.

> Therefore, the Julai [the Buddha Tathagata; also means, "a true immortal"] in his great compassion, let the secret making and melting be made known. He teaches one to re-enter the womb and create anew the inner essence and animated life of the ego; he shows how spirit and soul (vital

> breath) enter the germinal vesicle, how they must combine to become a unity in order to complete the true fruit, just as the sperm and soul of father and mother entered this germinal vesicle and united as one being in order to complete the embryo. The principle is the same.

We need to understand that the wise monk and Baynes are talking about a movement out of essence into matter, and then out of matter back into essence. Or, we may think of this as out of pure energy into matter and then back out of matter into pure energy. In order to do this, we need to be clear about the Chinese words and their equivalence in English (or *approximate* equivalent). My Chinese colleague, excellent meditator, and leader of Edgar Cayce activities in China, Cui Weidong, helped with these terms:

Jing in Pinyin (*Ching* in Wade-Giles) is a form of *qi* (*chi*) manifested in sexual fluids. Some consider this to symbolize the male's role in conception—energetically projecting sperm.

Qi (*Ch'i*) is vital breath, vital energy, *pneuma* (the vital spirit, soul, or creative force of a person); as such it is the life-force. Some consider this to symbolize the female's role in conception—providing the receptive egg inside the safety of the womb.

Shen (*shen*) is the divine, most refined form of *qi* (*chi*).

Usually, *Jing-qi-shen* (*Ching-chi-shen*) is used to describe three different conditions or stages, as: *jing* (*ching*) is physical, *qi* (*Ch'i*) is the life energy, and *shen* is the divine condition or stage. These three words reveal the secret process. We unite our animated life with our inner essence in the womb of mind and heart, so that our divinity is born again and our lower mind and physical body are spiritualized.

With these words in mind, the wise monk is using outer-life copulation between a man and woman to conceive a new baby as an allegory that reveals how similar the process is to achieving our *spiritual* rebirth. We re-enter the womb of our *deeper* heart and mind, and there we combine our spirit and soul to conceive our new "body." In ancient Egypt it was taught that in order to give birth to our divine "star body" (*akh*) we have to unite our essence or spirit (*ka*) with our animated soul (*ba*), then the "star being" (*akhu*) is conceived and brings into being our true, eternal self.[129]

Edgar Cayce, from his attunement to the Universal Consciousness, to the Mind of God, taught that not only God is God, but each of us is a part of that Oneness.[130] We need to awaken to our divinity and our role with the Divine Essence of all life. Then, we need to integrate this divine nature with our humanity in order to fully realize our potential and mission in this life and beyond.

Cayce taught that it is not all of life just to live it, nor all of death just to die—we must use these conditions to apply ourselves in growing wiser, stronger, and become a master over impulses, urges, and karmic patterns.[131]

Jesus actually addressed the need for this change from such a predominantly human focus to a more spiritual focus when he told Nicodemus that we must be *born again*. (See Endnote 34.)

Let's go back to the wise monk's teaching.

> Within the germinal vesicle is the fire of the ruler [spirit with will]; at the entrance of the germinal vesicle is the fire of the minister [mind]; in the whole body, the fire of the people [the cells of the body, each with inner essence and animated life]. When the fire of the ruler expresses itself, it is received by the fire of the minister. When the fire of the minister moves, the fire of the people follows him [spirit wills, then mind moves, then the cells respond]. When the three fires express themselves in this order a man [person] develops. But when the three fires return in reverse order the Tao develops. This is the reason that all the sages began their work at the germinal vesicle in which outflowing had ceased. If one does not establish this path, but sets up other things, it is of no avail. Therefore, all the schools and sects which do not know that the ruling principle of inner essence and animated life is in this germinal vesicle [remember, it is an invisible cavern of consciousness and vibration, having no form], and which therefore seek it in the outer world, can accomplish nothing despite all their efforts to find it outside.

This teaching that the germinal vesicle is *within* us and not outside of us fits with many Western teachings, including biblical teachings:

"Behold, the kingdom of God is within you."[152] The Disciple Paul asked in 1 Corinthians: "Don't you know that you are a temple of God, and that the Spirit of God dwells in you?" and "Don't you know that your body is a temple of the Holy Spirit which is in you, which you have from God?"

From Edgar Cayce's tuning to the Universal Consciousness, he too saw and taught that our bodies are more than physical vehicles for living in this world. Keep in mind that Cayce considered "God" to be the Universal Consciousness, the Creative Energy, the Life Force, a pervading Spirit that gives and sustains all life, so when he uses the word God he is speaking of the Infinite Eternal source and sustainer of all, the origin and destiny of all. Here are five brief excerpts:

"Know that your body is the temple of the living God; there you may seek communion. There you may seek counsel as to the choices to be made, the directions to be taken."[133]

"He has promised, 'If you will but open the door of your consciousness, of your heart, I will enter and abide with you.' This is not a fancy; this is not hearsay. You may experience such. For it is the law, it is the way, it is life itself!"[134]

"Seek and you shall find. Not without but from within. For in your own temple He has promised to meet you."[135]

"All that you may learn of the Father God, is already within self. For your body is indeed the temple of the living God, and as you meet Him there you may gain in your own consciousness the satisfaction of walking and talking with Him . . . When these consciousnesses are yours and you are one with Him, then indeed may you see that the kingdom of heaven dwells within."[136]

"This is a promise to you, to each soul; yet each soul must of itself find that answer within self. For indeed the body is the temple of the living God. There He has promised to meet you; there He does. And as your body, your mind, your soul is attuned to that divine that answers within, so may you indeed be quickened to know His purpose; and you may fill that purpose for which you entered this experience."[137]

For all of his teachings about seeking the origin and destiny within our body temple, Cayce always *balanced* this with many teachings about how our *outer* thoughts, words, and actions must support our *inner* seeking. If they don't, then the resulting hypocrisy brings dis-ease in the mind and body. If allowed to continue, it brings *disease*.[138] A person must be consistent within and without. Jesus Christ indicated this in the scene with the Samaritan woman at the well when he said: "God is spirit, and his worshipers must worship in the Spirit *and in truth*."[139] Of course, we must seek union in our spirit *with* the Spirit, but we also must *live* this belief in our thoughts, words, and actions with others and ourselves, daily. That is what the phrase *and in truth* means.

Patanjali taught the same in his *Yoga Sutras*. Our bodies are excellent physical vehicles but they are also secretly designed for *metaphysical* activity. All we have to do is learn the centers and pathways within the body that raise the vibrations and expand the consciousness, and budget the time to engage these.

The primary teaching throughout the wise monk's lessons is that individual life, individual consciousness, expressions, and activity *consume* the life force and *narrow* awareness and understanding. What each of us needs to do is *budget time* to plug back into the origin and source of inner essence and animated life. By doing so, we reunite with our Source and are renewed. Our life force is revitalized, revivified, and our mind awakens to an expanded awareness and a higher, wiser perspective. This is the goal of cessation of the outflow. It is not the loss of individualized inner essence and animated life, but *union* (the true meaning of the Sanskrit word *yoga*) of the individual with its universal source. It is the reunion of the finite with its infinite origin. This is the goal, and the rest of the teaching is guidance on how to do this—using specific physical practices (such as breathing and moving energy), maintaining better mental conditions (gathering the runaway thoughts, centering them, and stilling the mind), and understanding the secret truths.

2. The Six Periods of Circulation in Conformity with the Law

If one discerns the beginning of the Buddha's path, there will be the blessed city of the West. After the circulation in conformity with the law, there is a turn upward towards heaven when the breath is drawn in.

When the breath flows out energy is directed towards the earth. One time-period consists of six intervals (*hou*). In two intervals one gathers Moni. [(RW: *Sakyamuni*) *Buddha Moni*, the "Bringer of Light," therefore, this could be understood to be "gathering Light."] The great Tao comes forth from the center. Do not seek the primordial seed outside! [Here the circulation of the light/breath diagram appears in the original text. See it in this present book on p. 4.]

Now we focus more on the breath practice of inhaling and exhaling, but before we develop this, let's address the wise monk's instruction: "Do not seek the primordial seed outside!"

Many mystical sources teach this concept:

"Stand still and know that I am God, and that I dwell *within* you."[140]

"Seek first the kingdom of God *within* you."[141]

"Remember, the Lord your God is ONE! Your experiences through the earth then are one. The activities of your body, your mind, your soul SHOULD be then as one. And each experience to your self comes as those influences that make for regeneration, uplift, the experience which if taken into the activities of self becomes as the means for bringing harmony and peace in the inner self. Turn *within* and not without, as the inclinations are at times when your disturbances arise; and know that He has promised to meet thee in your temple. And your body IS the temple of your soul, the temple of the living God. And there He has promised to meet you. And His promises are sure, if you will but allow yourself to draw upon them in joy alike as in sorrow, in the ups as well as the downs. For He your God is not a God of wrath, nor of hate, but a God of love; for He IS love. And not only in your distresses praise Him, thank Him, but be consistent in your experiences, in your seeking; and you shall find that your relationships and your tendencies that arise—even from the unitarian forces in your own activities—may bring that which will not be the extremes. For the natural tendency is to go to the extremes. And the entity is oft very much elated over what? That which is bubbling as it were from within, that which is growing as from within. For remember, as you sow so shall you reap. And when that you have sown in your mind (for your mind is the builder) has grown to fruitage it brings that you have sown; some sixty, some forty, yea some an hundredfold. For a kindness, a gentleness to a fellow person brings more harmony into self than some great deed that may be well spoken of. For this is soon forgotten, but the fruits of the spirit—as may be experienced in your daily life—become as wells of living water, springing up within your self to bring that joy, that harmony that comes from walking oft with Him."[142]

I remember when I first started to meditate and how strange it was to seek within myself. During my early attempts at meditation I would search for the "Kingdom Within" as Jesus taught, but only find me—the little me! But I kept practicing. One day something within me "shifted" and I felt myself opening to another part of my consciousness. I was both surprised and *scared*. As the meditation practice continued, this grew into an inner awareness quite different from outer consciousness. One of the chief characteristics of this inner awareness was a "knowing," what we may call intuition—knowing as from out of nowhere! An understanding just came to me—not in words or sounds, just "knowing," true "cognition." The more I practiced, the more it grew and extended into my outer consciousness. My dreams also became more vivid and relevant.

Back to the original text:

> The most marvelous effect of the Tao is the circulation in conformity with the law. What makes the movement inexhaustible is the path. What best regulates the speed are the rhythms (*kuei*). What best determines the number of the exercises is the method of the intervals (*hou*). [The path is circular, the rhythms are the inhalations and exhalations, and the intervals are natural to our autonomic nervous system, both sympathetic and parasympathetic. In *ancient* China *kuei* (pronounced *gway* also *gwee*) meant *reversal, return,* and *renewal*, but here the term is used as "returns" or "turns" and associated with "rhythms." *Hou* means "time," and here is used for "intervals." However, in the ancient diagram, it refers to the lower chakras which live in time, both present and ancient (via karma).]
>
> This presentation contains the whole law, and the true features of the Buddha from the West are contained in it. [In mystical teachings from ancient Egypt to modern times, the East is the rising or the beginning of the long journey of the "sun" as our light being, and the West is the end of the journey, the final stages of the long journey. The East is our birth into this world and the West is our exit. That is why the Egyptians called the East the "land of the living" and the West the "land of the dead," meaning the "living dead" for they are beyond this world and all its distractions and illusions.] The secrets contained in it show how one gets control of the process by exhaling and inhaling, how the alternation between decrease and increase expresses itself in closing and opening, how one needs true thoughts in order not to deviate from the way, how the firm delimitation of the regions makes it possible to begin and to stop at the right time.
>
> I sacrifice myself and serve man, because I have presented

fully this picture which reveals the heavenly seed completely, so that every layman and man [persons] of the world can reach it and so bring it to completion. He who lacks the right virtue may well find something in it, but heaven will not grant him his Tao. Why not? The right virtue belongs to the Tao as does one wing of a bird to the other: if one is lacking, the other is of no use. Therefore, there is needed loyalty and reverence, humaneness and justice and strict adherence to the five commandments [The Buddhist five commandments are: 1) not to kill; 2) not to steal; 3) not to commit adultery; 4) not to lie; 5) not to drink and not to eat meat]; then only does one have the prospect of attaining something. But all the subtleties and secrets are offered in this *Book of Consciousness and Life* to be pondered and weighed, so that one can attain everything in its truth.

As I explained earlier, all ancient temples and schools held secrets closely and carefully. In the Asian world they taught that the Bird of Paradise has two wings; one wing is the right training and technique, which the wise monk has shared with us. The other wing is the *right heart*, or, as the wise monk referred to it, *the right virtue*. The Bird of Paradise doesn't fly with only one wing. All disciples must also have the right heart, the right virtue, for "the subtleties and secrets" that the wise monk has shared with us will not produce enlightenment and spiritual rebirth. With this teaching in mind and with Cayce's that I shared in Endnote 106, I always objectively searched my heart for my true motivation for seeking enlightenment and spiritual rebirth. Whenever I found myself carrying a little too much self-exaltation or egocentric thinking, I stopped seeking and spent more time in prayer and reading Scripture. It was my way of getting my heart right and my ego set aside. On those occasions when it was unusually difficult to get my heart right, I would look for opportunities to mundanely and physically help others with material life, letting go of my arrogantly superior sense of being "holier than thou, wiser than thou." I would not speak openly about spirituality, as if I knew much about it. Humility, meekness, and outer activity that helped others became my focus. I will add that Cayce's teaching about karmic reactions do not have to occur if we honestly process them in our hearts and minds openly with Universal Consciousness, the mind of God. I would not hide my arrogance from God and the collective consciousness, but reveal it and ask for help transforming it. Fortunately, this approach never failed me.

3. The Two Energy–Paths
of Function and Control

There appears the way of the in-breathing and out-breathing of the primordial pass. Do not forget the white path below the circulation in conformity with the law!

Our central nervous system has both gray matter and white matter. The white has been called the "subway of the brain and spinal cord" because messages move very fast through white matter. Since the breathing that is taught here uses the cerebrospinal system (brain and spinal cord), the wise monk wants to keep in mind that not only is breath being cycled during this method but beneath visualized breathing is actual bio–electrical energy moving through our body temple. The monk's use of the "conformity with the law" is a reference to Nature's intended purpose for white matter, thus our movement uses the natural activity of this matter.

Always let the cave of eternal life be nourished through the fire! Ah! Test the immortal place of the gleaming pearl! In the text there is another picture here which is very similar to the first. It shows again the paths of energy: the one in front leads down and is called the function-path (jen), and the one at the back leading upwards is the control-path (*tu*).

This picture is *really the same* as the one that precedes it. [See the diagram of the circulation of the light/breath p. 4.] The reason that I show it again is so that the person striving for cultivation of the Tao may know that there is in his own body a circulation in conformity with the law. I have furnished this picture in order to enlighten companions in search of the goal. When these two paths (the functioning and the controlling) can be brought into unbroken connection, then all energy-paths are joined. The deer sleeps with his nose on his tail in order to close his controlling energy-path. The crane and the tortoise close their functioning-paths. Hence these three animals become at least a thousand years old. [Here we have an exaggeration. Tortoises can live 400 to 500 years, but the oldest crane on record lived to be 83. Deer and Elk live from 6 to 14 years. Of course, the monk is using the concept of resting the function–path and the control–path, as well as closing them, to add longevity to animate life.] How much further can a man go! [The average lifespan for a human is 79 years, and the maximum is 115, according to *ScienceDaily*.[143]] A man [person] who carries on the cultivation of the Tao, who sets in motion the circulation in conformity with the law, in order to let inner essence and animated life circulate, need not fear that he is not lengthening his life and is not completing his path.

I have used this "circulation of the Light" breath for many years now. It is truly an energizing, uplifting way to enhance the Life Force within us. When I do this breath cycle, I begin with inhalation from my root chakra (my mind's eye visualizes my energy and breath in the region of the sexual organs at the base of my spine); as I inhale I imagine, feel, and experience drawing energy up to the top of my upper chakras in my brain (pineal, hypothalamus, and pituitary). Here I imagine, feel, and experience the *macrocosmic* Breath of Life joining with my micro-cosmic, raised breath. I feel my life force merge with the universal life force. I abide here in this merger. Then, as I exhale I *bathe* my body and spiritual centers with this united, descending energy anterior to my spine—running through the center of my body all the way down to my root chakra. Here I sit in the empty breath. At first my body became uncomfortable, and was even concerned about my staying in the empty breath. But eventually it relaxed and trusted that I was going to take another breath before passing out. The empty breath is a place of deep stillness, and stillness is a condition that allows the Creative to awaken. Then, I repeat the cycles of inhalation and exhalation. I know that this breathing path is not natural to us, and many have shared with me that they thought inhalation should draw in energy and exhalation should expel it. But this method is "back-flowing," a reversal of the body's natural way. It is internal and follows the teaching of *reversing* the normal flow of life (and breath) for the purpose of gaining higher consciousness and revivifying energy.

Edgar Cayce adds a left-brain, right-brain breath also raising our personal life force and unites it with the infinite, universal Life Force: using the right and left nostrils he alternates the energy between the left brain (right nostril) and the right brain (left nostril).[144] We inhale through our right nostril, drawing in "strength" (imagine this, feel it, and experience it), and then exhale through the mouth in a controlled, slow exhalation. After lots of practice you will have better control of your diaphragm. When you gain better control, full, deep inhalations and steady, slow exhalation will be easy to do, and very pleasant. Cayce suggested that we do three of these. Next, we do three inhalations through the *left* nostril but exhale through the right nostril, not through the mouth. When doing these inhalations we are to imagine, feel, and experience opening the spiritual centers of our body. This breath is felt more in the head than in the torso, and is more gentle than the "strength" inhalations. I combine this breathing method with the Taoist one, and find they both enhance the life force within my body temple, adding to my soul's comfort and increasing its presence. Even when I'm not going to meditate, I will do these breathing methods to help my body.

4. The Embryo of the Tao

According to the law, but without exertion, one must diligently fill oneself with light. Forgetting appearance, look within and help the true spiritual power! Ten months the embryo is under fire. After a year the washings and bathings become warm. [The washings and bathings are the inhalations (washings) and exhalations (bathings).]

This picture will be found in the original edition of the *Leng Yen Ching* [Picture here was, "Stage 3: Separation of the Spirit-body for Independent Existence" see pp. 14–17. But the ignorant monks who did not recognize the hidden meaning and knew nothing about the embryo of the Tao have for this reason made the mistake of leaving this picture out. I only found out through the explanations of adepts that the Julai [a true immortal] knows real work on the embryo of the Tao. This embryo is nothing corporeally visible which might be completed by other beings, but is in reality the spiritual breath-energy of the ego. [Here it is helpful to understand that there is a higher ego or higher Self; as well as a lower ego or self-centered self, so natural to our lower nature.] First the spirit must penetrate the breath-energy (the soul), then the breath energy envelops the spirit. When spirit and breath-energy are firmly united and the thoughts quiet and immobile, this is described as the embryo. The breath-energy must crystallize; only then will the spirit become effective. Therefore, it is said in the *Leng-Yen-Ching* [see endnote 59]: "Take maternal care of the awakening and the answering." The two energies nourish and strengthen one another. Therefore, it is said: "Daily growth takes place." When the energy is strong enough and the embryo is round and complete it comes out of the top of the head. This is what is called: the completed appearance which comes forth as embryo and begets itself as the son of the Buddha.

A soul born *into* this world comes out at the bottom of the mother's torso, but a resurrected spiritualized "body" comes out of the top of the head — the fontanelle or soft spot in a baby's skull, the crown chakra. In mystical lore it is thought that most people exit, "die," through the solar plexus portal in the human body, but a spiritualized person exits, "dies," through the portal of the crown chakra, the top of the head. It appears that the wise monk is aware of this idea. In sleep, which is the shadow of death, and in meditation, which is a death–like experience, a spiritual seeker's soul may exit through the crown, and return through the crown.

In my journey with this practice, the phrase "comes out of the top of head" is real. I actually feel my spirit energy and soul rise and expand upward and out of my body into the infinite and universal out of the finite and individual. They never disconnect. In fact, the finite and infinite become one, the individual and the universal become one. I wrote a book about this practice and method called, *Passage in Consciousness*, which details the various stages in the passage from finite awareness to infinite awareness, from individual *being*–ness to universal oneness, with diagrams and illustrations.[145]

5. The Birth of the Fruit

Outside the body there is a body called the Buddha image. The thought which is powerful, the absence of thoughts, is Bodhi. [This is a Sanskrit word meaning "Awakened" or "Enlightenment," which leads to liberation from the cycles of incarnate lives.] The thousand-petalled lotus flower opens, transformed through breath-energy. Because of the crystallization of the spirit, a hundredfold splendor shines forth.

The picture here is "Stage 1: Gathering the Light"; see the illustrations of the stages in in this present book pp. 14–17. Notice that the wise monk has these stages out of sequence; it may be assumed that he knows what he's doing.

In the *Leng-Yen-Ching* [see endnote 59] it is said: "At that time the ruler of the world caused a hundredfold precious light to beam from his hair knots." In the midst of the Light shone the thousand petalled, precious lotus flower. And there within the flower sat a transformed Julai [Self]. And from the top of his head went ten rays of white, precious Light, which were visible everywhere. The crowd looked up to the out-streaming

Light and the Julai [a true immortal one] announced: "The
divine, magic mantra is the appearance of the light-spirit,
therefore his name is Son of Buddha."

If a man does not receive the teaching about inner essence
and animated life, but merely repeats meditation formulae
stolidly and in solitude, how could there develop out of his
own body the Julai [a true immortal], who sits and shines
forth in the lotus flower and appears in his own spirit-body!
Many say that the light-spirit is a minor teaching; but how can
that which a man receives from the ruler of the world be a
minor teaching? Herewith I have betrayed the deepest secret
of the *Leng-Yen-Ching* in order to teach disciples. He who receives this way rises at once to the dark secret and no longer
becomes submerged in the dust of everyday Life.

Here is a subtle but important teaching: True reflection is finding the
center in the midst of conditions. All Light emanates from the center. The
mind must be still. But stillness without the Light is *not* illumination.
Stillness *with* the Light is illumination. The warning is this: What has
to be changed by *reflection* is the self–conscious heart. If today people
sit and meditate looking only at their own egos, and call it reflection,
how can anything come of it? All our efforts and methods and skill
must eventually include the Light, otherwise we are simply meditating with our self–consciousness, which will not lead to illumination
and liberation. Although the way to illumination is quite simple and
easy, there are so many *transforming* and *changing* conditions connected
with illumination that we must set self aside and patiently go through
all the transitions, but do so *with* the Light. Cayce supports this: "For
remember, ever, that Mind in its entirety is ever the Builder. For it is
step by step, line by line, precept upon precept, here a little, there a
little, that the attaining is accomplished in the mental, the spiritual, the
material applications of an entity in this material world."[146]
Cayce adds to our search for the Light: "For in the beginning, God
said, 'Let there be light.' You [Ms. 5367] are one of those sparks of light,
with all the ability of Creation, with all the knowledge of God."[147]
Within us is this original spark of light so intimately one with the Light.
Jesus indicates this when he tells Nicodemus that "no one ascends to

heaven but he [and she] who first descended from it,"[148] and then tells the disciples that they know where he is going and they know the way![149] Cayce adds: "Not only God is God but ... self is a portion of that Oneness . . . "[150] He explains: "This requires that expression then, in time and space, of that patience of which He spoke, 'In patience become you aware of your souls.'"[151]

Reflection is not thoughts. Reflection is centering on the origin of Life. Only the inner essence that has existed since the beginning can overcome the illusion. The biggest tip that I can give to another seeker is make sure that your heart contains a *genuine* desire to unite inner essence with animate life. There is a universal law: *seek* and you will *find*. Just be sure that you are not seeking for self-exaltation or power, but with an attitude of cooperation, humbleness, and enduring patience.

When that illumination comes, know that there is another law: as you receive, so must you give. "Do that [he's referring to seeking the Light by helping others] and live a normal life, and you'll live a heap longer; [and] be worth a heap more than the position you occupy. For it is not what you do but what you *really are* that counts. This shines through—*what you really are*—much more than what you say."[152]

We then need to share the Light, even with those sitting in darkness who cannot appreciate our treasure. But we do this not by preaching or naively exposing our pearl of wisdom to ridicule. The very presence of the Light within us affects those around us—consciously and unconsciously.

6. Concerning the Retention
of the Transformed Body

It is one thing to conceive and birth the separate body,
it is quite another thing to retain it. Here the wise monk
begins the lesson on retention.

> Every separate thought takes shape and becomes visible
> in color and form. The total spiritual power unfolds its traces
> and transforms itself into emptiness. Going out into being
> and going into non-being, one completes the miraculous
> Tao. All separate shapes appear as bodies, united with a
> true source.

Cayce taught that we originally entered the material as *thought
forms*, not flesh bodies. Gradually, we pushed our way deeper into
matter, and it resulted in our becoming encased in material bodies.
Here's Cayce:

> "When souls sought or found manifestation in ma-
> teriality by the projection of themselves into matter as
> became thought forms and when this had so enticed the
> companions or souls of the Creator, first we had then the

creation in which 'God breathed into man (God-made)
the breath of life and he became a living soul,' [Genesis
2:7] with the abilities to become godlike. Hence, we find
the first preparation . . . or manner in which those souls
might through material manifestation acclaim—by the
living, by the being—that which was and is and ever
will be consistent with the purposes of creation—was
given into the estate of man [humanity]. The entity was
among those first who through those channels came
into consciousness, awareness of the relationships of
the material man to the Creative Forces; that came into
material activity during the early portions of man's
CONSCIOUSNESS of being an independent entity, or
body, in a material existence. Thence we find the entity
passing through those experiences, becoming rather
aware, with the sons of those activities in the experiences when all thought forms in matter were put away
through the experience of Noah."[153]

There were actually *four* creations or stages. The first was as expressions within the infinite essence and in the image of this infinite
essence, found in Genesis 1. The second was into form with united
yin-yang (first as thought forms, but eventually encased in material
bodies). This is the being formed from the "dust of the earth" creation,
found in Genesis 2. The third was in gender-specific bodies, separat-
ing yin and yang (with the complementary portion retained behind
the veil or in the unconscious portion of our minds), found in Genesis
2:18-25. This ultimately led to the Children of God gradually pulling
away from oneness with Infinite Eternal, and becoming increasingly
isolated in this dimension of life, resulting in their leaving the Garden
where they abode with God, as found in Genesis 3:22. But things didn't
get better, they actually got worse. The Creator and Nature felt the
growing willful destruction and negativity in the now lost Children of
God. Material life had become out of sync with celestial, heavenly life,
and the Creator and Nature were moved to cleanse material life and
start over, as found in Genesis 6. After the cleansing came the so-called
Second Creation, which is our current condition—highly physical with

dynamic separation between the celestial and terrestrial, the spirit and the flesh, our essence and animated matter. Now we begin the long journey to reawaken the original consciousness. A mission to reestablish the condition of life as it was—once upon a time so very long ago. These lessons in Taoism contain the way to enlightenment, liberation, and reunion.

7. The Face Turned to the Wall

This section of the lesson is about formlessness, vital emptiness, and reuniting with the pure, original portion of our being.

> The shapes formed by the spirit-fire are only empty colors and forms. The light of inner essence shines back on the primordial, the true. The imprint of the heart floats in space; untarnished, the moonlight shines. The boat of life has reached the shore; bright shines the sunlight.

Cayce touches on this, stating that through *deep meditation* we will come to not only *see* the light but may enter in and *become a portion* of the light.[154] He gave a little affirmation that could be used as a mind–centering mantra. This is one line: "Let the light of Your countenance be only that as may come to me now." Depending on our various individual understandings toward terminology associated with the Divine, we may think of the word "Your" in this affirmation as God or the Infinite Source of essence and life, or simply the wise monk's "spirit-fire." Spirit is often expressed as fire, even in the Bible. For example, when John the Baptist described his powers versus the powers of Jesus, he said: "I baptize you with water [for the cleansing of sin]; but he who is mightier than I is coming . . . he will baptize you with the Holy Spirit and with fire."[155] Another example is when Jesus brought the Holy Spirit upon those gathered around him, it was described as tongues of fire: "There appeared tongues of fire, distributed and resting on each one of them. And they were all filled with the Holy Spirit."[156] Jesus described God as a spirit: "God is a Spirit: and they that worship him must worship in spirit and truth"; then the Disciple Paul wrote that this spirit is a fire: "Our God is a consuming fire."[157]

Obviously the Taoist meditators were experiencing the original, true essence as a spirit-fire. In this passage the monk taught that the effect of the spirit-fire was to cease the passions of the heart (the heart floats); the personal self is untarnished (symbolized as moonlight—that portion of us that is *reflecting* the light, but not the source of light); the animated portion of life (the boat of life) finds the shore of the essence; and the source of light (the sun) finally shines bright again.

I experienced a similar contact with the sun in a deep meditation in an Egyptian temple. My tour group and I sat on the hard, cold stone floor in a very special chamber inside an ancient Egyptian temple. We began to still our minds and bodies for meditation. The guards at the temple were laughing and talking in Arabic; the echo of their voices was so great inside the temple that it was very difficult to meditate. However, rather than give up or get angry I asked myself, "When was I ever going to get back to this temple?" I told myself that I had to succeed *now*. Then, I tried with all my might to filter out their voices and get into deep meditation. It worked. It worked so well that I not only lost consciousness of the voices, I completely lost consciousness of the temple and my group, and found myself entering into a vivid ancient Egyptian ceremony. It was an initiation ceremony involving water and fire. I found myself standing shoulder-deep in a pool of holy water, naked. Somehow, I knew this was a purification ritual. As I walked up the stone steps out of this sacred pool, attending priests wrapped a floor-length cape around me. Then they anointed my head with oil and combed my hair back. My hair was black and thick with sacred oil. Two of them approached and handed me the two scepters of Egypt, the crook and the flail. I intuitively knew that if I wanted to move, I held them out in front of me, and to stop, I crossed them over my chest. I looked up and saw two lines of ancient Egyptians in front of me—a row on my left and a row on my right. I tilted the two scepters toward them, causing me to glide across the floor, not walk, glide just an inch above the floor. It was an exhilarating feeling to glide so effortlessly. The two long rows were composed of priests and gods. I glided between them. They nodded their heads and smiled approvingly. At first, I thought this was approval but soon I realized that it was also a nod of encourage-ment to continue through the next phase of the initiation. I looked up ahead of them to see what was at the end of the rows. To my amazement and concern, it was the Sun, the real Sun! At the end of this column of priests and gods, I was to enter the fire of Ra. But this Ra was the *real* Sun that would burn me to ashes. I looked hard into the eyes of the priests and gods, expressing to them with my eyes my deep concern about this part of the initiation. They smiled and nodded with more enthusiasm than before. I knew that all I had to do was cross the scep-ters and I would stop. But within me was a longing to experience the whole initiation, so I kept the scepters pointed straight toward the fiery Sun. As I entered it I felt the searing heat, but instead of burning me, *it cleansed me!* Just as the Disciple Paul had described, God was a consum-ing fire. The Ra fire was burning away all my sins and weaknesses but not harming the rest of me. So happy was I that I began to draw its heat into me, inhaling it, wanting more of it. It felt wonderful! I wanted it to burn me completely, thoroughly, until I was fully cleansed! Suddenly, someone grabbed my arm and began shaking me saying, "John, wake up, you're going to miss our bus. We have to go. Wake up!" I struggled to see through the Sun's brilliant light. Two faces were staring back at me, they were our Egyptian guide and my colleague in this present life. I asked, "Who are you?" They both looked at each other and then turned to me and ordered me to get up and follow them closely, and to not say anything that would alarm the guards and others in our group. I obeyed, gradually realizing that I was supposed to be a part of this tour group, yet half of me was still in the initiation ceremony. Once on the bus, I fell back into the solar cleansing. Oh, it felt so good to be so clean! For nearly a year after this experience I could go back into this cleansing initiation by simply entering meditation. Gradually over time, it faded, but with a little effort I could bring it back again as if I never left it. This was my first deep meditation experience with the spirit-fire and its power to change.

Cayce taught that there are many negative influences that we must shield ourselves from before entering deep meditation. Some of these are of our own karma from earthy habit patterns of thought and behavior. Some of them are dark influences in the macrocosm. Either way, it's best to shield ourselves prior to entering deep meditation. Here is one of Cayce's teachings on this. The parenthetical and italicized comments are Cayce's, brackets are mine:

"When an individual then enters into deep meditation: It has been found throughout the ages (INDIVIDUALS have found) that self-preparation (to THEM) is necessary. To some it is necessary that the body be cleansed with pure water, that certain types of breathing are taken, that there may be an even balance in the whole of the respiratory system, that the circulation becomes normal in its flow through the body, that certain or definite odors produce those conditions (or are conducive to producing of conditions [incense]) that allay or stimulate the activity of portions of the system, that the more carnal or more material sources are laid aside, or the whole of the body is PURIFIED so that the purity of thought as it rises has less to work against in its dissemination of that it brings to the whole of the system, in its rising through the whole of these centers, stations or places along the body [plexuses and chakras]. To be sure, these are conducive; as are also certain incantations, as a drone of certain sounds, as the tolling of certain tones, bells, cymbals, drums, or various kinds of skins [membranes stretched over one or both of the open ends of a drum]. Though we may as higher thought individuals find some fault with those called savages, they produce or arouse or bring within themselves—just as we have known, do know, that there may be raised through the battle-cry, there may be raised through the using of certain words or things, the passion or the thirst for destructive forces. Just the same may there be raised, not sedative to these but a CLEANSING of the body. 'Consecrate yourselves this day that you may on the morrow present yourselves before the Lord that He may speak through YOU!' is not amiss. So, to ALL there may be given: FIND that which is to YOURSELF the more certain way to your consciousness of PURIFYING body and mind, before you attempt to enter into the meditation as to raise the image of that through which you are seeking to know the will or the activity of the Creative Forces; for you are RAISING in meditation actual CREATION taking place within the inner self!"[158]

I took this to heart: "you are raising in meditation actual CREATION taking place within the inner self." Therefore, I was always careful and conscious of my vibrations, emotions, thoughts, and attitudes *before* entering into deep meditation. If these were not ideal, then I would contemplate what are the impulses that are influencing my present condition and how might I modify them. I would pray so as to subdue or even alleviate the negative influences. To enter into meditation with these negative influences would give power to them, for meditation gives strength to whatever is held in the mind and heart.

8. Empty Infinity

Without beginning, without end, Without past, without future. A halo of light surrounds the world of the law. We forget one another, quiet and pure, altogether powerful and empty. The emptiness is irradiated by the light of the heart and of heaven. The water of the sea is smooth and mirrors the moon in its surface. The clouds disappear in blue space; the mountains shine clear. Consciousness reverts to contemplation; the moon disk rests alone.

In my personal experiences with the Golden Flower teachings and Cayce's deep meditation training, all methods, stages, techniques, images, and sacred words lead to an expansive, enlivened stillness and revivifying emptiness. This condition is non–being, non–active, *yet* it contains the vibrant essence of life. In the early stages it is like sitting in the breath of the Infinite Eternal and its soft rhythms of inhalation and exhalation. In the latter stages it is like sitting in perfectly pure oneness, unmoved, and without motivation to move—absolute peace and contentment.

When in this deep meditative condition, I feel actively *imbued* with the Quintessence of the Infinite Eternal. As this increases, I become *one with* the essence, and my beingness disappears, joyfully. Abiding in this condition motionless, without thoughts, there's a peace that comes over me. I desire nothing. My breathing becomes so very shallow that I am barely breathing. My body and mind are happily still. There is a magic in this state. I can sense that something special is happening but it is often subtle.

At some unknown timing, I come out of this condition back into individualness, but now I'm sublimely imbued with the essence of the Infinite Eternal.

It is difficult to retain this condition when back in the world of people and activities, including my own human feelings and thoughts. Despite this, its effect never seems to leave me. My outer self may get far from this condition, but there is always a lingering remnant within me that never goes far away. And despite all of my outer self's interests and desires, I never lose my longing to unite with that non-being, inactive condition. Therefore, I budget time in my busy life and the dynamics of my relationships with others for meditation time, especially for deep meditation times. It makes me a better person and I have a better perspective.

Here is the image that the original manuscript had at the ending of this section on Empty Infinity:

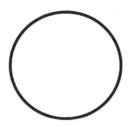

Additional Cayce Teachings

Here are further teachings in Cayce's vast collection of discourses. You may find these to be helpful in your meditation practice and in daily life. His teachings are categorized using a number system, making it easier to find a specific comment in the massive collection. I have provided the numbers for those of you who want to access the teachings. If you are a member of Cayce's organization, you can go to the website EdgarCayce.org, log in, click the link "Search the Readings," and then search the collection using these numbers or any words or phrases relevant to what you are looking for.

Soul

Let's begin with the teachings about the nature of our soul.

"The soul cannot die; for it is of God." (262-85) "The soul will never die." (294-7)

Cayce was asked, "What is the soul of a body?" to which he answered, "That which the Maker gave to every entity or individual in the beginning, and which is seeking the home again or place of the Maker." (3744-1)

"The soul is the real self, the continuous self. The mind is the builder, continuous to the extent that it is constructive, taking hold upon spirituality in such a manner and way as to become constructive—and that which is constructive and good is continuous. Hence we find the body—physical—subject to the laws of the physical being, or the temperaments, the environments, the disappointments, the activities throughout; and all of these act both physically and mentally." (1620-1)

In the following teaching he reveals how we have two bodies. One is the physical, clay body, and the other is a subtle inner body that is the dwelling place of our spirit or soul.

"That which is of the earth–earthy; that channel, that house, that piece of clay that is motivated in material forces as the dwelling place of the spirit or the soul—that is the superficial body. The soul body is the motivative power within, that has either grown in the constructive forces in its associations or activities, or to the gratifying, satisfying of the superficial emotions or urges." (262-85)

As with so many wisdom teachings, Cayce states that actions must reflect beliefs, or we are hypocrites. "You BELIEVE that your body is the temple of the living God. Do you act like that? Then begin to put same into practice, making practical application of that you have gained, LEAVING the results with your God." (262-82) We'll see more of this teaching in the next section of Cayce's interpretation of the Revelation.

Mind

Now let's look at Cayce's teachings about the mind. "Mind ever is the builder; hence man in the mental sphere, man in the material sphere, must make for that experience where the Body and the Mind are as one and not warring one with another; so that the consciousness of the Spirit of Truth is ever the motivative influence in the experience of the individual in its activities." (262-88)

Cayce identifies the first cause for our existence as: "That the created would be the companion for the Creator." This is the reason we were created, and as a result, the created (our soul) is given opportunities to "show itself to be not only worthy of, but companionable to, the Creator." (5753-1)

Since our true self is eternal, immortal, he suggests the following:

"Don't put the material first, for you have to live with yourself a long, long while! Become acquainted with yourself. Know yourself and the relationship to the Creative Forces." (3484-1)

He taught a lot about *feeding* our mind and soul as we do our body. "Fill self's mind with those things that create more and more a unison of CREATIVE thinking, whether this be as applied to material, spiritual, or purely mental and social relations. Be sure they are CREATIVE in their essence." (303-2)

"Remembering ever, mental law in mental application; spiritual law in spiritual application; and that MATERIAL conditions are the OUT-GROWTH of the application of each; for MIND the builder; the spirit the creator; the material that created. Great truth! Keep it before you." (900-374)

The Body's Spiritual Centers

According to Cayce, a portion of our soul is woven into our bodies. Edgar Cayce's extraordinary teaching is in reading 281-38: "The glandular forces then are ever akin to the sources from which, through which, the soul dwells within the body." And he expands on this, saying, "It may be easily seen, then, how very closely the glands are associated with reproduction, degeneration, regeneration; and this throughout—not only the physical forces of the body but the mental body and the soul body."

The following is Cayce's layout of the endocrine glandular system (281-29) and its relationship to various energies, such as the light spectrum. I have listed the glands from higher to lower. He identified the three upper glands as "heavenly" and the four lower as "earthy."

Pituitary: color *violet*, musical note *ti*, planet *Jupiter*, bodily region *forehead* and *frontal lobe* of the brain, influence is *strength and spirituality*, church in the Revelation *Laodicea*;

Pineal: color *indigo*, musical note *la*, planet *Mercury*, bodily region *crown* of the head (fontanelle) and center of the brain—Note: the pineal gland has features found in our eyes—cones and rods for seeing; so it may be the "third-eye" center as well. However, the group working with Cayce gave that honor to the pituitary. After my many years of deep meditation and research, I'm inclined to accept the pineal as the third eye and the influence that opens the crown chakra. Its influence is *mental* and *memory*, church in the Revelation is *Philadelphia*;

Cayce taught that the 24 Elders in the Revelation correlate with the 12 paired cranial nerves, of which the vagus nerve descends into the body. Thus, from here on Cayce identifies the plexuses associated with the glands and chakras. He encouraged seekers to get massages and adjustments to keep these plexuses properly aligned and the energy flowing through them.

Thyroid: color *blue* or *gray*, musical note *so*, planet *Uranus*, bodily region *throat* and the *cervical* plexus (particularly C3), influence is *will* and psychic ability, church in the Revelation is *Sardis*.

Now we enter the earthy chakras, so Cayce correlates each with one of the four beasts found in biblical prophecies, notably Ezekiel, Daniel, and the Revelation. He also identifies them with the earthly elements: earth, water, fire, and air.

Thymus: color *green*, musical note *fa*, planet *Venus*, region of the body *chest* (note: the heart chakra is not the pump but the gland) and the intercostal nerves of the somatic nervous system (particularly T4), influence *love* and *righteousness*, church in the Revelation *Thyatira*, of the four beasts in the biblical imagery this gland is the *eagle*, of the four elements this is *air*;

Adrenals and pancreas: color *yellow*, musical note *mi*, planet *Mars*, region of the body *abdomen* and the *solar plexus* (particularly T9), influence *temperament (anger)* and *forgiveness*, church in the Revelation *Pergamon* (Pergamos), of the four beasts this is the *lion*, of the four elements this is *fire*;

Cells of Leydig (named after German anatomist Franz Leydig, Cayce called this the lyden center): color *orange*, musical note *re*, (pronounced *ray*) planet *Neptune*, region of the body these are mostly found in spaces in and around male *testes* but also in spaces in and around female *ovaries*, Cayce associated them with the *navel chakra*, and they are reflectively stimulated via *pelvic plexus* and lumbar region (particularly L4), influence *mysticism* and *guidance*, church in the Revelation is *Smyrna*, of the four beasts this is *"one like unto a man,"* of the four elements this is *water*;

Gonads (testis or ovary): color *red*, musical note *do* (pronounced *doe*, as in baby female deer), planet *Saturn*, region of the body *lower abdomen* and the *pelvic plexus* and lumbar region (particularly L4), influence is *bodily needs*, church in the Revelation *Ephesus*, of the four beasts this is the *calf* (remember Aaron's golden-calf mistake), of the four elements this is *earth*.

Much of this information is found in Cayce's 281 series of teachings about the Revelation and how it correlates to the body temple. See the next section of this book for a little more on Cayce's symbolic interpretation of the Revelation and its relevance to our spiritual journey.

Know Thyself

Let's view his teachings about the classical directive to "Know Thyself." The following teachings are found in 262-10. I have paraphrased this teaching for easier reading and better focus on the topic at hand.

He encouraged us to study self in its *relation to others*. Literally, stand aside and see self pass. Take the time to be occasionally introspective of what may happen in self's relation to others, to see the reaction of others to what was done by self; for no man lives to himself and no man dies to himself.

Take into account the acts, thoughts, and words for the day, for these reflect your concept of God. Would you act before God as you do your brother? "A new commandment I give unto you, that you love one another." Dare to realize that you now, today, begin to reflect a full development of your soul, that you now manifest God's love and are known before man as you are known of God. Self only stands in the way. Then begin to study and discipline self, that your words and actions may not be so different that they are not children of the same family.

Who is my mother, my brother?

In seeking to know self through meditation, or taking inventory of self, one is passing, as it were, a signpost, seeing a little, catching a word here, an idea there, from those we contact day by day, which shows we are all closely related and are traveling along the same road. Truly therefore, in knowing self is knowing the other person also, for all are parts of one mind. Should it not make us more tolerant of the weakness of our brother as we view him as we are, or as we have been? Service being the means of fulfilling our mission here, the question will naturally arise, Am I doing all that I can for my brother? Am I giving freely of self to help others? Is every moment of my life lived as He would have me live? Am I a channel of blessings to others? (262–10, paraphrased)

We Are Star Travelers

We are star travelers according to Cayce, children of the infinite universe. The portion of ourselves that survives death of our physical body, our soul-self, is a true star traveler, as we find in this Cayce teaching:

"As an entity passes on from this present time or this solar system, this sun, these forces, it passes through the various spheres –leading first into that central force known as Arcturus—nearer the Pleiades on and ON through the EONS of time, as called, or space. Eventually, as an entity passes into the inner forces, inner sense, then they may again—after a period of nearly ten THOUSAND years—enter into the earth to make manifest those forces gained in ITS passage. In entering, the entity takes on those forms that may be known in the dimensions of that plane which it occupies, there being not only three dimensions—as of the earth—but there may be seven as in Mercury, or four in Venus, or five as in Jupiter. There may be only one as in Mars. There may be many more as in those of Neptune, or they may become even as nil—until purified in Saturn's fires." (311–2)

"As the entity moves from sphere to sphere, it seeks its way to the home, to the face of the Creator, the Father, the first cause." (136–8)

Why Do We Suffer?

Cayce addressed why so much of life in this world contains suffering, heartbreak, and confusion. Like so many of the ancient teachings around the planet, illusions must be seen for what they are and dispelled. This is often painful for the outer, earthly self but brings forth of the inner, eternal self—the true self. Cayce asked us all: "How CAN it be then that you do not understand God loves you?" Sensing our doubting this, given that our lives are not always happy, he asked and answered: "Why do you suffer? It is mercy, it is justice to your soul! For those things that are cares of the flesh and of the earth cannot inherit eternal life. Hence life alters, life changes in the experiences of individuals through their sojourns in the Earth, and thus you learn your lessons, even as He; for though He were the Son, though you are His sons and daughters, yet must YOU learn obedience through the things that you suffer." (262-100)

I've paraphrased this next teaching for ease of reading.

Self must open the door that He may enter in. Self will work at that job of bringing that consciousness, that awareness of His presence in the material and mental affairs of life, knowing that lesson must ever be that the spirit is the life, the mental is the builder, and the physical or material results are the effects of the application of the knowledge or understanding toward life, light, or the spirit of ANY effort. So, then, measure self and self's efforts by that standard in Him who went about doing good. Do you likewise. (262-28)

Free Will

Here are some Cayce teachings on free will.

Many of Cayce's teachings call for us to use our God-given gift of free will. Yes, of course we have karma that shapes our fate, but even in the midst of karma we the ability use our wills—if only for determining with what attitude we meet our fate.

Cayce often taught that we must do something—right or wrong, but do something; make a decision and do it. He explained that in the doing comes the understanding. Many of us have learned much from mistakes, and we now say something like, "been there, done that, not going there again." That indicates that we are wiser now than we were before we did that. In the doing comes understanding and soul growth. Consider this teaching: "By what powers does a grain of corn maintain its ability to produce corn; that divine gift to the first corn? By not try-ing to be something else than a grain of corn! Thus may there come an understanding to any soul, to any that will say 'Use me, O God, as You will.' But not remaining idle! For, as has been given, ACTIVITY IS the key to understanding. Rather had there be a purpose or an act in error than no act. For movement is the effect of spirit. Spirit is life. But let the inner self, the divine self, the knowledge of same be directed only by Him." (705-2)

"And what makes for the change? WILL! What, then, is WILL? That which makes for the dividing line between the finite and the infinite, the divine and the wholly human, the carnal and the spiritual. For the WILL may be made one WITH HIM, or for self alone. With the Will, then, does man destine in the activities of a material experience how he shall make for the relationships with Truth. What is Truth? That which makes aware to the inmost self or the soul the Divine and its purposes with that soul." (262-81)

Setting Ideals To Live By

One of Cayce's frequent teachings was about setting and living by an ideal.

"As you contemplate, as you meditate, as you look upon the Mind, know the Mind has many windows. And as you look out of your inner self, know where you are looking, [where] you are seeking. What is your ideal? What would you have your mind-body to become?" (262-78)

"The first injunction as would be to the entity: Know what is thy ideal. Know innately within self what ye desire to do. Then most of all be honest with thine own self. Never do in a mental or physical or spiritual manner ANYTHING that is to self questionable, or to which ye yourself may even put a question mark. This does not indicate, nor instruct one to be goody-goody. Far, far from it! Rather be good FOR something, and be ACTIVE. Better to do even the WRONG thing than to do nothing. Remember, the man given only one talent hid it, and he it was that was questioned—he it was from whom it was taken—even that which he seemed to have. Hence that necessity, especially within self in the present, to be fair and honest, and without question to self. Let others think as they may. Let others speak or rant as they may—but as for self, satisfy thine own conscience as to doing that which is just and right." (674-3)

The Power and Importance of Music

"Music is of the soul, and one may become mind and soul-sick for music, or soul and mind-sick from certain kinds of music." (5401-1)

"Music alone may span the distance between the sublime and the ridiculous. Between spirit and body, mind and soul." (3253-2)

"Music is that which spans the distance between the finite and the infinite. Keep the music, for it is oft a help to thee to quell the storms of life." (3179-1)

"Do learn music. It is part of the beauty of the spirit. For remember, music alone may span that space between the finite and the infinite." (3659-1)

I have found significant bridging using music created by Karunesh. Two songs on Karunesh's album titled *Zen Breakfast* helped me. The first song helped me stimulate and enliven my spiritual centers, it is titled "Moon Temple." The second song titled "Calling Wisdom" took me to the high-mountains places of the mind! On his album titled *Call of the Mystic*, the song "Ancient Voices" also helped me cross that bridge to a higher place of being. He has many albums and songs. I have them all, but these that I mentioned have worked for me. I believe that his spiritual understanding, musicality, and mindful *intention* imbues his music with the powers to lift me to higher levels of consciousness and vibrations.

I have also found this bridge using a few classical pieces of music, but none of the classical "relaxation" albums. Surprisingly, I have not found a bridge using new age music either, but that could be because *my* soul's innate vibes are not moved by such. Some spiritually motivated *vocals* have been very helpful, such as chanting and choral music.

Chanting

The physical body is uniquely designed for both physical activity and higher mental, and spiritual activity. There are three primary sound chambers in the human body: the abdominal chamber in belly area, the cardiopulmonary chamber in the chest, and the cranial chamber in the skull. Sounds can be directed toward these chambers and the resonance of these sounds changes the vibrations of atoms, cells, and organs. These sounds also affect the mind-body connection, raising consciousness throughout the nervous system.

Cayce's chanting methods use the voice and breath to vibrate select sounds in these three chambers and the seven spiritual centers to improve health, well-being, and enhance enlightenment.

Chanting is inner sounding rather than outer singing. The sound of the voice is directed inward rather than outward, as one does when singing. Directing the sounds to the three major chambers with resonance and in a droning manner, one can truly effect a change in vibrations and consciousness.

As we've seen, Cayce gave insights into how chanting was used in the ancient Egyptian temples, particularly the Temple Beautiful. He said to use an incantation or chant that "carries self deeper—deeper—to the seeing, feeling, experiencing of that image in the creative forces of love, entering into the Holy of Holies within you. As self feels or experiences the raising of this, see it disseminated through the inner eye to that which will bring the greater understanding in meeting every condition in the experience of the body. Then, listen to the music that is made as each center of your own body responds to that new Creative Force."

Cayce's chanting is God-centered, meaning that it seeks to attune the chanter to the divine source of life. He taught that such attunement naturally results in greater health, happiness, well-being, and enlightenment.

Chanting begins by sounding in the abdominal (belly) chamber of the body—the root, navel, and solar plexus chakras. Then the sounding shifts to the cardiopulmonary (chest) chamber—the heart chakra and even into the throat chakra. Finally, the sounding is to move into the skull (head) chamber—the frontal lobe of the brain, and the third-eye and crown chakras.

The chants are not just given for attempting to raise and transform bodily vibrations. Each chant is designed to lift and carry the mind and spirit to higher, more harmonic levels of attunement to the divine, to that Oneness within which all life exists. Usually, the first series of chants are devoted to raising the vibrations of the body, then, as the body energizes, the next round of chanting lifts the consciousness or mind from lower areas to higher, even into the Infinite Consciousness of God's mind.

For example, when chanting Cayce's ar-e-om chant, the ar sounds are directed into the abdominal chamber and the lower chakras—like this: ar–ar–rrr. As the sound changes to the e, one directs the vibrations of the voice to the upper portion of the abdominal chamber to the solar plexus area in the center of the torso, like this: eeee. Then, as we shift to the O sounds we move our minds and vocal vibrations to the heart chakra in the cardiopulmonary chamber and to the throat chakra, where the voice box is, like this: oooo. The next stage is a bit different from most classic yoga teachings, which would direct the sounds straight up to the crown of the head. Rather, Cayce instructed us to move the sounding to the base of the brain, then over to the center of the brain, and ultimately to the large frontal lobe of the human brain. For example, in the third phase of the chant these sounds would shift gradually from oooo (ohhh) in the chest and throat to uuuu (ooh) at the base and center of the brain, and then shift easily into the mmmm sound in the frontal lobe. This area affects the master endocrine gland of the human body, the pituitary, with the hypothalamus adjoining it. Hold the mmmm sound and feel your body and mind shifting from their normal, everyday condition to a more centered and divinely attuned condition.

Thus the Cayce chant would be: ar–ar–rrr– eeee–oooo– uuuu–mmmm. In order to get the full effect of this power incantation, one needs to take a deep breath and save some breath for the last sound, which is the most important sound, because it awakens the highest spiritual centers.

You will need to take a three–level breath. Let me explain: In order to fill your lungs, you need to inhale near your diaphragm, by expanding your belly, then inhale further by expanding your chest, and then still further by lifting your shoulders as you inhale. Now your lungs are full. As you sound the chant, control the release of your breath by controlling your diaphragm—gradually passing the breath through your vocal cords. With practice you'll be able to do a good, long chant.

An often overlooked but very important part of chanting is the silence that follows the sounding. Don't immediately inhale and chant again. Use the silence between chants to imagine and feel that your body, mind, and soul are rising to higher levels of vibration and consciousness. Ultimately, chanting leads to the deep silence of oneness with the indivisible Source of Life. There you abide silently as you are imbued with health, well-being, and enlightenment.

Using Affirmations

Of all the wonderful guidance to come through Edgar Cayce's attunement to the Universal Consciousness, using an affirmation to change one's mind, mood, health, perspective, abilities, and reach for new potentials is a unique Cayce idea. He gave over 100 affirmations to people seeking physical, mental, or spiritual help.

"By affirmation, we mean that it should BE an AFFIRMATION! ... Not merely spoken in a singsong manner or said just once. Take at least the time to repeat the affirmation, POSITIVELY, three to five times that there may be the full, POSITIVE response in the mental activities of the body." (271-4, paraphrased)

From Cayce's perspective, an affirmation is an ideal structured in a potently suggestive statement. He instructed us to speak (aloud or silently) the affirmation, being sure to maintain a consciousness of the meaning of the words, and to speak it with a positive, expectant attitude until the whole of our mental being is affected positively by the meaning. He suggested that the affirmation be repeated three to five times, and the goal is to achieve a "full, *positive* response" from the mental portion of our being.

I have selected three of his affirmations, which are printed at the end of this section. The first one was intended to take hold of desires, needs, and attitudes that we all experience in life and move them to a higher, more universally attuned condition, resulting in greater harmony and happiness in our lives. After shaping this affirmation, Cayce sharply instructed the person to "leave it with Him" rather than to keep wondering and doubting, in anxious waiting for immediate results. He wanted people to feel the power of the affirmation in their mental self and then let it go free. The reason for this, he said, was that the "unseen forces," more powerful than the seen, work in a different way. The unseen forces work best when we have faith in them, a demonstrated faith shown by allowing them to work their magical way through our bodies, minds, hearts, and lives. He said that the spirit of patience, expectancy, and contentment are fertile soil from which the unseen forces can bring forth their miracles.

The second affirmation was designed to help a person find the best ways to be a channel of blessings to others. Cayce explained that the phrase "my going in and my coming out" (taken from Exodus 28:35) is speaking about going in to the holy place within us, where God meets with us, and coming out from that holy place to interact with others and our outer work. The going in is mostly done during sleep, prayer, meditation, and moments of reflection and stillness.

The third affirmation was designed to connect us with what Cayce called "the Christ Consciousness," a state of mind and perspective that best channels the power of light and love into and through us—an excellent state to be in. If you are not Christian or have had some bad experience with Christianity, in one reading Cayce used the term God-Consciousness as a synonym for Christ-Consciousness. The term Christ is simply the Greek language version of the Hebrew term Messiah. Both literally mean "anointed one." I find it helpful to think of Christ as the personal conscious contact point for each of us within the vast, infinite, impersonal God of the Cosmos. They are one and the same, but the Messiah is that promised direct-connection point that God gave to the prophet Daniel through the archangel Gabriel (the first time the term Messiah appears in the Bible).

In addition to meditation times, affirmations are excellent mantra-like thought-centering sayings to use throughout the day, especially when challenges appear or one is feeling down, unhappy, unsure, or stuck. They're also great ways to sing the joys and thanksgivings when life is good!

Here are three of Cayce's suggested affirmations. The language has elements of King James Bible English. You can change these to fit our modern wording.

"Let my desire and my needs be in Thy hands, Thou Maker, Creator of the universe and all the forces and powers therein! And may I conform my attitude, my purpose, my desire, to that Thou hast as an activity for me. And leave it with Him, and go to work!" (462-8)

"Lord, here am I! Use Thou me in the ways as Thou knowest best. May my going in and my coming out always be acceptable in Thy sight, my Lord, my Strength, and my Redeemer." (2803-3)

"Let that mind be in me that was in Him, who knew that of Himself He could do nothing, yet in the power of the light of the Father of all may we, may I, may all, come to know His love the better. Thy will, O Father, be done in me just now." (436-3)

Using Incense

Ancient temple ceremonies and initiations attempted to alter sensory input for the purpose of affecting higher consciousness using sounds, music, and chanting, as well as light, flame, images, and mandalas. Selected foods and flavors worked through the taste buds. Oils, lotions, and certain animal skins and fabrics affected consciousness through touch (e.g., the Egyptian priests and priestesses wore leopard , and the Mayans wore jaguar). And incense was and continues to be used to alter consciousness through the olfactory nerves, the sense of smell.

It's important to remember that the objective is not to stimulate the senses into heightened physical awareness but rather to amplify awareness of the ethereal, the infinite, the spiritual by altering the input coming through the five senses.

Edgar Cayce's insights on the origin, power, dangers, and usefulness of incense are helpful. Here's a good reading to consider (I've edited it for clarity and focus on the point of our study):

"From what did the plant obtain its ability to produce in the one that of lemon, in another orange, in another lavender, in another violet? From its parent stock which was given, not by man but by the Creative Forces. Yet, man has the ability to take and make that which becomes as an essence that responds to or sets in vibration the olfactory influences in the mucous membranes of the body of a person. There is the ability to make odors that will respond to certain individuals and groups; and many hundreds are responding to odors that produce the effect within their systems for activities in which the Creative Forces or God may manifest in the individual! For odor is gas, and not of the denser matter that makes the degrading things." (274-10)

Careful consideration of the influence will help us determine the scents that are best for us. When asked what incense was best, Cayce often referred to the person's past lives. For example, though he often recommended sandalwood incense, in one soul's reading he strongly warned against it, because that soul had used the incense in a past life for heightened sexual pleasure. One person's spiritual scent may be another's physical distractor. This means that each of us has to study, test, and intuit the scents that lift us into higher vibrations, higher states of consciousness.

Here are a few of Cayce's comments to various people seeking help with selecting an incense:

"As to the manner of meditation, then: Begin with that which is oriental in its nature—oriental incense. Let the mind become, as it were, attuned to such by the humming, producing those sounds of o-o-o-ah-ah-umm-o-o-o; not as to become monotonous, but 'feel' the essence of the incense through the body-forces in its motion of body. This will open the kundalini forces of the body. Then direct same to be a blessing to others. These arise from the creative center of the body itself, and as they go through the various centers direct same; else they may become greater disturbing than helpful. Surround self ever with that purpose, 'Not my will, O God, but Thine be done, ever,' and the entity will gain vision, perception and, most of all, judgment." (2823-3)

Here's another of his teachings:

"Q: What kind of incense should I use during meditation?

"A: Cedar. And hyssop." (275-39) [In the Bible, hyssop was sprinkled on celebrants at sacred ceremonies.]

"Hence those things oriental, those things that deal with subtle odors, subtle activities upon those senses of individuals, play their part in the experience of the entity; not sandalwood, but—cedar surrounding the entity will bring a satisfaction; and in the burning of same, in the odors of same, may the entity harken back to much of the developed mental abilities of the entity." (346-1, notice the past-life harkening)

Interestingly, Cayce tells this woman that using this incense will help her to find the right balance in "relationships to individuals, to itself, and to solving problems." Then he tells her to "always burn three, when such is done." I don't know why he said this, but the number three reflects the dimensions of this world and the trinity, which Hinduism also holds as God's nature—triune nature: physical, mental, and spiritual.

Here are four more short clips from readings suggesting scents for meditation and ceremony:

"Lavender, odors that come from come from sandalwood have a peculiar influence upon the body in the present; for these bespeak of something innate within self that bespeaks of the abilities of the

soul, mind, and body to revivify and rejuvenate itself as to an ideal."
(587-2)

"The odor of the peach blossom or of those natures partaking of the
sandalwood as combined with same." (1058-1)

"The odors of sandalwood or orris [iris] and violet are well; for
these, when the entity meditates, create an environment for the entity."
(1616-1)

"As we have indicated to the entity, there must be some ceremony.
Choose whatever manner that befits thine own consciousness, whether
this is from odors or otherwise. And if odors are chosen, choose sandalwood and cedar to be burned." (2175-6)

Personal choice is the key for Cayce, as in this next reading that also
warns about becoming too dependent upon external help.

"If the self or soul self comes to depend too greatly upon external
influences ...then it is not self-development. And self-development in
its relationship to the Creative Forces ... is ever the better. For, each soul
must come to know its OWN influence and that which is the most helpful. And if it calls then for self to cleanse the body without and within
with pure water, or to fast, or to burn incense, or to set about self certain
odors or colors of influences, then... use these" (440-12)

Here is a fascinating insight:

" Did lavender ever make for bodily associations? Rather has it ever
been that upon which the angels of light and mercy would bear the
souls of men to a place of mercy and peace, in which there might be
experienced more the glory of the Father . . . Hast thou ever known the
odor from a flesh body of a babe to be the same as the odor from a
body that has been steeped in the sins of the world, and has become
as dross that is fit only to be cast upon the dunghill?" (274-10)

Finally, here's a reading that take us beyond the physicality of incense and into the ESSENCE of incense.

"Q: Do I have any special psychic ability, and if so how is the best
way to use it?

"A: As indicated, especial psychic ability—and the way to develop
same is in the manner as indicated. Know that which MOVES the
mental, the spiritual, the physical. Do not confuse same, but through
the intonations from kinds of music or colors ye may attune thyself.
But know to WHAT ye are ATTUNING! For even as the incense in the

holy of holies was not the power of God, but rather the attuning of the finite mind to an infinite expression—be NOT overcome with the material expressions but seek rather that as He hath given, 'I will meet thee within thine own self.'" (1695-1)

This next reading reveals how much our past lives affect our present. Note how lotus, sandalwood, and cedar can almost overwhelm this lady today, even though their influence comes her ancient incarnation in Egypt.

"Before that [incarnation] we find the entity was in that land now known as the Egyptian, among those that came from what is known as the Atlantean land and with the Atlantean, when there were the incoming of many that dealt much with the building up of those experiences in spreading the truths that had been set as tenets for the lands of many. … From that experience, in the present the entity finds that there is a peculiar innate feeling when certain dress or certain type of dress is seen, and that colors and odors have a peculiar effect upon the entity. And when there are the lotus and the sandalwood with cedar they become almost, even yet to the inner senses, overpowering." (504-3)

Edgar Cayce's Interpretation of the Revelation and Its Relevance to the Golden Flower

Edgar Cayce approached the biblical book of the Revelation most closely to the traditional *symbolic* interpretation. But he saw beyond the symbolism of earthly matters, seeing the text filled with *metaphors* of mental and spiritual processes. In fact, Cayce taught that the whole Bible is more than a historic record of humanity's physical journey with God and with one another; it is also an allegory of *metaphysical* activities and influences. And as an allegory it contains hidden teachings, insights, lessons, and instructions concerning the origin, growth, and destiny of our souls, which are nonphysical. And it is both a microcosmic view in which the story is very personal to each individual soul, and a macrocosmic view in which all souls are involved as a soul group. For example, he taught that the biblical Adam did not only represent an individual soul but *an entire soul group.*[159] He taught that our souls were among that group, a group called in the book of Job the "Morning Stars." Here's that text:

"Then the Lord answered Job out of the whirlwind, saying . . . 'Where were you when I laid the foundations of the Earth? Tell me, if you have understanding . . . Who laid the cornerstone, when the *morning stars* sang together, and all the sons [and daughters] of God shouted for joy?'" (Job 38:1–7) Later in this conversation God actually answers His question for Job: "Do you know, for you were born then? Or because the number of your days is great?" (38:21) The animated portion of our projected being was born long, long ago, when the Creator laid the foundations of physicality, and we have had many incarnations in matter and beyond.

Our souls were alive long before this incarnation and will live long after it. According to Cayce, the Bible tells the story of our souls' journey (individually and as a group) from our creation in the image of God, through the fall from grace and the loss of the Garden, up through the struggles to regain that glory that was ours "before the world was." (EC 1158–9 and John 17:5) The Revelation, according to Cayce, is a very special part of the great biblical story and should be studied as a kind of roadmap for the final spiritualization of our bodies and minds to fully reach our intended purpose for existence: eternal companionship with our Creator.

The psalmist wrote: "I say, 'You are gods, sons [and daughters] of the Most High, all of you. '" (Ps. 82:6) And even Jesus addressed this: "Is it not written in your law, 'I said, you are gods?' If he called them gods to whom the word of God came (and scripture cannot be broken), do you say of him whom the Father consecrated and sent into the world, 'You are blaspheming,' because I said, 'I am the Son of God'?"

The symbols and scenes in this last book of the Bible represent experiences and stages through which *we* pass in *our* struggle to awaken again spiritually and regain our close connection with God and the Garden we once shared. Cayce says that some symbols and places in the Revelation actually represent *glands* within our bodies and *thought patterns* within our minds. (EC 1173–8) In his own words he explains: "the visions, the experiences, the names, the churches, the places, the dragons, the cities, all are but emblems of those forces that may war within the individual in its journey through the material, or from the entering into the material manifestation [i.e., physical body and this world] to the entering into the glory, or the awakening in the spirit . . ." (EC 281–16)

This is quite a unique approach to the Revelation. Most interpreters believe that it is a story about the forces in the outside world. Cayce acknowledges that it does have that content, but its greater purpose and message is to each individual soul as a map of the spiritual path we travel *within* our bodies and minds to reach the ultimate purpose for our being: oneness and companionship with our Creator, and with one another (the two great commandments). For Cayce, the outer struggle is important, but the inner work is the key to understanding the message in this mysterious manuscript. "The symbols," he says, "represent SELF; self's body-physical, self's body-mental, self's body-spiritual . . . and they are ONE in you—even as the Father, the Son, and the Holy Spirit is one in Him." (EC 281-16)

Why then was it written in such a cryptic manner? According to Cayce, it was to keep its spiritual secrets for "those that were, or will be, or may become," through their spiritual seeking, initiated into an understanding of "the glories that may be theirs if they will but put into work, into activity," the guidance and calling found in the text of the vision. As the Spirit comes to each church and speaks to them, so Cayce wants each of us to ask ourselves: "What is lacking in self? Are you cold? Are you hot? Have you been negligent of the knowledge that is yours? Are you stiff-necked? Are you adulterous in thought, in act, in the very glories that are yours?" (EC 281-16)

In every line of the Revelation, every activity, every symbol, we find good and evil engaged in a struggle. This struggle, according to Cayce, is within our hearts and minds, and is because we were created to be heirs, joint heirs with Messiah/Christ/Logos, as sons and daughters of God, to that everlasting glory that may be ours. But the material, physical forces, and self-satisfying interests take strong hold of us, and we forget our spiritual destiny. Yet, Cayce does not see the physical as evil or a stumbling-block to spiritualization; rather as a tool, a stepping-stone to aid in our spiritual struggle if we use it properly, as the Revelation reveals. Even the ancient *Yoga Sutras* convey this truth: the human body is not only an excellent vehicle for physical life and three-dimensional consciousness; it is an excellent device for experiencing metaphysical life and spiritual consciousness.

Here are some examples of Cayce's interpretation of symbols, scenes, and characters found in the Revelation:

The Seven Churches: These represent the seven spiritual centers within the body. In classical Hinduism and Buddhism these centers are called *chakras,* which means "wheels," spinning wheels of energy located in specific areas of the human body. Cayce correlates these centers to the endocrine glands, which secrete the powerful hormone messages directly into our bloodstream, affecting all parts of our body. (EC 281–29) Each of these churches represents a specific spiritual center. The virtue and the fault of each church symbolize the virtue and fault of that spiritual center within us. These powerful centers affect the soul and mind inhabiting the body. Therefore, the Spirit moves through each church, calling on it to overcome its weaknesses and to do what it knows to do, so that the final glory may be achieved. This initial process involving the spiritual centers within our bodies is intended to help prepare us for the spiritualization of our minds and hearts described in subsequent chapters of the Revelation.

The Seven Lamps of Fire: These represent the helpful influences that destroy hindrances to the spiritual awakening. They are inner messengers, aids, who stand between the forces of good and evil and become as powers within our human nature to overcome, and allow our divine nature to more fully be expressed. (EC 281–29) This idea may be an extension of the teaching that angels watch over us. An example of this can be found in Psalm 91:11 "For he will give his angels charge over you, to keep you in all your ways." It may also be the power of our inner conscience that helps us along the way. But with Cayce, it may also be our inner thoughts and chemistry: What thoughts and hormones are we releasing most often? Those that fire up the carnal or earthly forces of the body or the gentler, calmer, more uplifting ones, that make our body a temple for our soul?

The Four Beasts: These are the four fundamental physical natures (desires) of our earthly, human nature that must be subdued. They are also the four destructive influences that "make for the greater desire for the carnal forces." (EC 281–29 and –16) The Revelation's description of each adds to our understanding of these forces and how we may control or at least reduce their negative qualities. These also represent urges and forces in the four lower, more earthly endocrine glands in our bodies. Cayce equates the four lower glands with earthly forces and the three upper glands with heavenly forces. There will be more on this in a later chapter.

The Great Red Dragon: This symbolizes that powerful urge within ourselves that originally so separated us from the Source of Life that we would fight with those very influences that would bring about the spiritual awakening we seek. The Great Red Dragon is the serpent from the Garden in Genesis (Rev. 12:9) who first aided in our souls' separation from God's presence and the Garden—symbolic of a serpent-like willfulness and reasoning within ourselves, when we were heavenly "teenagers with the keys to the car." Now this influence has grown strong and powerful in the form of a great, red dragon, ready to devour any new, heaven-centered intentions we bring forth in our hearts and minds. (EC 281-16)

Mark of the Beast: This strange mark, *666*, represents vows and obligations we have made to the work of the Beast and how we condemn rather than help any effort to overcome the Beast's influence. The Beast is like our selfish ego and egocentric interests. It represents the work of self alone, without our Creator's influence. The mark is erased when the work of our hands and thoughts of our minds are cooperating with God, rather than simply being self-driven. The Beast is our lower nature at our most selfish, self-centered, self-gratifying, self-glorifying point of existence.

New Heaven and New Earth: These represent a new heart/mind and a new body. Throughout the Old Testament you may have noticed that the Lord makes occasional reference to giving us new hearts or "circumcising" our hearts. (Deut. 10:16, 30:6; Eze. 18:31, 36:26; Jer. 4:4) Here, in the final book of the Bible, we have received our new hearts. These also represent a new vibration in the seven spiritual centers. The "wheels" are spinning with a new purpose, a new life-force; one that is spiritualizing. Therefore, we have a new body, too. One that helps the heart and mind maintain higher consciousness.

Water of Life: This is the transformative, rejuvenating influence of the Spirit of God flowing through our purposes, which have been made pure in "the blood of the Lamb—which is in Jesus, the Christ, to those who seek to know His ways." (EC 281-37) Ingesting this water is cleansing, making us new and reborn. But, once again, it is not actual water that we are talking about. It is the essence of water from within us, as Jesus meant when he said, "He that believes on me [the "me" here is Spirit abiding within the man Jesus], as the Scripture has said, from within him/her shall flow rivers of living water," John 7:38. Jesus's reference to a passage in scripture is to Isaiah 58:11 where we find a similar comment about the inner water: "And the Lord will guide you continually, and satisfy your soul in dry places, and make strong your bones; and you shall be like a watered garden, and like a spring of water, whose waters fail not."

Tree of Life: This represents "the sturdiness of the purpose of the individual in its sureness in the Christ." (EC 281-37) The tree's leaves represent our *activities* that are as healings to others and ourselves in the material life. The fruits of this special tree are the "fruits of the spirit." Cayce listed them in many of his discourses as: kindness, patience, joy, understanding, gentleness, long–suffering, forgiveness, etc. The tree's ability to bear fruit each month indicates the continuousness of the influence of this sturdiness and these activities that bring forth the spiritual fruits in our lives.

Cayce's interpretation calls each of us to participate in a great struggle to be born again in the Spirit and spiritualize our lives, bodies, and minds.

In chapter 1 verse 10 of the Revelation, the apostle John tells us that he was "in the spirit on the Lord's Day." Cayce says that he meant that he was in deep meditation. (EC 281-16) In this deep state he was caught up in the Spirit of God and "turned" (Rev. 1:12) away from the outer world. He began viewing the inner, heavenly world, and was told to write what he saw and heard. Cayce says that what John perceived was for his own personal spiritual development as well as for other souls who, by their own development, could sense the true meaning of this story and its strange imagery, and use it to benefit their own journey. Again, the journey we are speaking of is the journey from being a predominantly physical, material being to a predominantly spiritual, celestial being, sojourning temporarily in the physical world.

Cayce's entire translation and guidance is found in my book: *Edgar Cayce's Amazing Interpretation of the Revelation*, available on Amazon.com.

Endnotes

1. In no way is my use of CE and BCE, "Current Era" and "Before Current Era," an attempt to remove Christ from the calendar. I am simply using these because they have become so commonplace in writings today and I am dealing with Chinese history and texts, which belong to the world of the Far East.

2. Again I want to state clearly that in no way is my use of the BCE and CE, "Before Current Era" and "Current Era," an attempt to remove Christ from the calendar. See endnote 1

3. Strong's #430—*The Exhaustive Concordance of the Bible*, generally known as Strong's Concordance. It is a Bible concordance indexing every word in the King James Version of the Bible (KJV), and was completed under the direction of James Strong, professor of exegetical theology at Drew Theological Seminary. It was first published in 1890.

4. Strong's Concordance #433

5. John 1:1–5

6. John 1:1–5, John 1:29–33, Luke 3:22

7. Edgar Cayce 900–181

8. Edgar Cayce 1158–12

9 Edgar Cayce 254–85

10. Gottfried Wilhelm Leibniz (1646–1716) was one of the great thinkers of the 17th and 18th centuries and is known as the last "universal genius." One of his key works was *The Monadology*, 1714, a short text which sketches in some 90 paragraphs a metaphysics of simple substances, known as monads.

11. Baynes's translation, page 6

12. Cleary's book, p. 3

13. Cleary's book, p. 5

14. https://open.library.ubc.ca/circle/collections/ubctheses/831/items/1.0089774

15. Nicholson, James Michael, The Huiming Jing: A Translation and Discussion, The University of British Columbia, Department of Asian Studies, Masters Thesis, December 2000, page 7. See url in note 14.

16. Olson, Stuart Alve *The Jade Emperor's—Mind Seal Classic*, Dragon Door Publications, St. Paul, MN, 1992, page 13.

17. John 14:6

18. Edgar Cayce 991-1

19. The ancient Egyptian gods Geb (earth) and Nut (sky) made love, and thereby produced the "World Egg" from which the sun was born in the form of a phoenix bird. From the womb of Nut, impregnated by Geb, were born the gods Osiris, Horus the Elder, Set, Isis, and Nephthys. Isis is referred to as "The Egg of the Goose," Geb being the "Great Cackler" or Goose. Through this we were all conceived as *goslings* of the Great Goose. And when it came to Ra, we were the *rays* of the great Ra (pronounce *Ray*, and some write it, Re).

20. John 14:10–11

21. Matthew 3:16

22. John 10:17

23. "The entity's ABILITIES lie in that direction of bringing aid and understanding TO others, through the gaining of that hope that ever lies within each individual, that may be awakened to that divine that is within EVERY entity of its relationships to its Creator or to the Creative Energies as may be manifest through a human soul." (6-2)–Edgar Cayce's reading number 6-2 for a 33–year-old female social worker. Cayce gave her soul's past lives as being a mediator between the Native Americans and Colonists (1620-1675), then a defender of Troy (1194-1184 BC, a female who unsuccessfully attempted to seek cooperation between Greeks and Trojans), then in early Canada at the ending ice age (circa 8000 BC), eventually moving south and becoming one of the Mound Builders, then in very early Egypt as a supporter of the High Priest Ra-Ta and a teacher and guide to the people (circa 10,500 BC). She may have had more incarnations, but these were the ones most affecting her current incarnation.

24. *Jade Emperor*, p. 41, see endnote 16

25. Thomas Cleary translated this opening passage as, "Naturalness is called the Way"; Walter Picca translated it as, "That which exist through itself is called Meaning (Tao)." As you can see, I prefer how the Wilhelm and Baynes editions translated it, which is: "That which exist through itself is called the Way (Tao)."

26. Genesis 2:7

27. Edgar Cayce 254-110

28. Matthew 13:33

29. John 3:13

30. Cleary is most critical of this translation by Wilhelm, stating that it means something closer to: "a spirit (i.e., mind) that is completely open and completely effective"—*zhixu zhiling zhi shen.* page 82 of Cleary's book.

31. Edgar Cayce 281–13

32. Edgar Cayce 281–38

33. Edgar Cayce 3969–1

34. John 3:3–13 "'That which is born of the flesh is flesh. That which is born of the Spirit is spirit. Do not marvel that I said to you, you must be born anew. The wind blows where it wants to, and you hear its sound but don't know where it comes from and where it is going. So is everyone who is born of the Spirit.' Nicodemus answered him, 'How can these things be?' Jesus answered him, 'Are you a teacher of Israel, and don't understand these things? Most assuredly I tell you, we speak that which we know, and testify of that which we have seen, and you don't receive our witness. If I told you earthly things and you don't believe, how will you believe if I tell you heavenly things? No one has ascended into heaven, but he who descended out of heaven, even the Son of Man, who is in heaven.'"

Notice in this last sentence how Jesus, who was the "Son of Man," is conveying that even though he is physically standing before Nicodemus, he is actually in heaven. This indicates that heaven is a state of consciousness, and can be entered from anywhere if the mind and heart are tuned to or conscious of heaven's essence. Notice also that no one ascends to heaven who did not first descend from heaven. A part of us has already been in heaven and descended into our baby body upon physical birth. Most of us have lost touch with this part as we became so focused on the physical outer world and our fleshly self, that we've lost awareness of our spiritual, godly self. Yet, it whispers to us. We sense that there is more to life than this. There is also a longing in us, a longing that nothing in this world can fully satisfy. We feel there is a missing portion of our being.

35. There were many magical seals used in ancient China. You may want to look into: "Taoist Seals—A Case Study of Correct Method of the Heart of Heaven", Researcher HO Hei Man, at Department of Fine Arts, The Chinese University of Hong Kong:
http://www.arts.cuhk.edu.hk/~fadept/?research-post=taoist-seals-a-

case-study-of-correct-method-of-the-heart-of-heaven. You should also consider this: *The Jade Emperor's Mind Seal Classic*—translated by Stuart Alve Olson, and published in English in 1992 by Dragon Door Publications. Actually, the title is more correctly titled, *Mind Seal* or *Book of the Seal of the Heart*, where the *Heart* is a heavenly *consciousness*, or a state of mind.

36. Edgar Cayce 3436-2

37. Here I changed Wilhelm's word "intelligence" to "mindfulness," for it better expressed the Old Master's intention.

38. Edgar Cayce 900-429

39. Edgar Cayce 3161-1

40. Edgar Cayce 262-24

41. Edgar Cayce 2030-1

42. John 14-17

43. In Genesis chapter one *Elohim*, in chapters two and three *Yahweh Elohim*, and in the rest of the book just the name *Yahweh*. Subsequent to these initial three names for God we find *Adonai* (the plural of *Adon*, again meaning "Lord" or "Master" or even "Owner") and *Jehovah* (A Latinization of the Hebrew *Yahweh*, also meaning "Lord").

44. Edgar Cayce 3484-1

45. "Women In Europe" (1927). In *Collected Works*, 10: "Civilization in Transition," page 254.

46. Tao by Matsumoto, Taoism videos, Chapter 10, E. Dark Depth Female at: http://taotechingdecoded.com/01to10/1000e.html Or, Search Google for „Dark Depth Female."

47. "The Doctrine of the Mysterious Female in Taoism: A Transpersonalist View," by Evgueni A. Tortchinov, Department of Philosophy, St. Petersburg State University, Russia. 2016

48. Matthew 19:14

49. Edgar Cayce 2475-1

50. The Divine Feminine is found in chapter 12 and the Whore of Babylon is found in chapter 17 of Revelation.

51. John 3:13

52. Luke 17:21, only in the King James version of the Bible, all others change this to "with you," but the KJV states clearly that it is "within you."

53. John 14:9-11

54. Edgar Cayce 364-10

55. 1 John 1:7

56. Edgar Cayce 364-6 and others

57. Edgar Cayce 281-13

58. Edgar Cayce 900-227

59. "The Structure and Dynamics of the Psyche," in *Collected Works* 8:157

60. [איתאד הניכש ימקמ סוקיא רמא הימאד אערכ לק עמש הוה יכ רסוי בר], from the Babylonian Talmud, Qiddushin, 31b.]

61. [אשריהמ הצדיקס מהש םהש סינכשמ השכינה בראץ.—from *Pesiqta Rabbati* 5.]

62. Edgar Cayce 294-202

63. Revelation 21:2, 9, 22:17

64. Revelation 20-22

65. Matthew 25

66. Hebrews 12:29

67. Cleary's translation, page 44, verse 24, and page 112, note 25

68. The *Leng Yen Ching*, is a Buddhist text dating to 705 CE. It teaches that the only way to overcome illusion and bondage is to obtain enlightenment. The master describes specific practices that enable one to reach the goal of liberation, which is freedom from the law of causality (karma).

69. Edgar Cayce 906-3

70. Edgar Cayce 386-2, my italics

71. Psalm 82:6, to which Jesus referred with his comments in John 10:34

72. Edgar Cayce 255-12

73. Edgar Cayce 3744-2

74. Edgar Cayce 255-12

75. Plato's *Symposion*, c. 385-370 BCE, and Aristotle's *Nicomachean Ethics*, 340 BCE

76. From their top-selling album *Rumours*, "Dreams" was Fleetwood Mac's only No. 1 hit in the USA in 1977. The song was written by Stevie Nicks at a turbulent time for the band. *Rumours* won the Grammy for Album of the Year. The spelling is because Fleetwood Mac was a British-American band, and British English was used.

77. This has nothing to do with the Old Testament, as some teachers claim. Jesus states that this is "often said," *not written* in the Scriptures. Jesus is not teaching that the Old Testament taught hatred. I have just quoted the Old Testament's statements on love that match the New Testament. In point of fact, consider this Old Testament teaching: "If you meet your enemy's ox or his donkey wandering away, you shall surely return it to him." (Exodus 23:4-5) And this one: "If your enemy is hungry, give him food to eat; and if he is thirsty, give him water to drink." (Proverbs 25:21) These Old Testament teachings clearly lead one to respect one's enemy. The Old Testament does *not* teach hatred of one's enemies.

78. Edgar Cayce 262-116

79. John 15:13

80. John 16:12

81. *Yinfu Jing* ("Book of Secret Correspondence") is also known as *Huangdi Yinfu Jing* ("Yellow Emperor's Book of Secret Correspondence"). It is said that *Yinfu Jing* was discovered by Li Quan, a famous Taoist of the Tang Dynasty (618-907) on Shaoshi Hukou cliff of Songshan Mountain (today this is the Henan Province). Basically, it teaches that a person should act in *accordance* with Nature. It also explains the correct usage of ears, eyes, and mouth, which follows the cooperating relation in the five elements to cultivate one's better self. *This* is the teaching that the Old Master is referring to in the passage we reading: "Release is in the eye."

82. *Huangdi Neijing*, literally the "Inner Canon of the Yellow Emperor" or "Esoteric Scripture of the Yellow Emperor," is an ancient Chinese medical text that is the fundamental doctrinal of Chinese medicine. The work is dialog between the mythical Yellow Emperor and six of his legendary ministers. The *Neijing* takes readers away from the old shamanistic beliefs that disease was caused by demons. It taught that the natural effects of diet, lifestyle, emotions, environment, and age are the reason diseases develop. It taught the universe is composed of various forces and principles, such as yin and yang, Qi (*chee*) and the Five Elements. A person can stay in balance or return to balance and health by understanding the laws of these natural forces. Each person is a microcosm that mirrors the larger macrocosm.

83. John 3:8

84. visit, https://www.health.harvard.edu/blog/mindfulness-medita-tion-may-ease-anxiety-mental-stress-201401086967

85. visit, https://www.health.harvard.edu/heart-health/can-deep-slow-breathing-lower-blood-pressure

86. Matthew 6:19-22

87. Philippians 4:7

88. Genesis 2:7

89. Edgar Cayce 262-15, 294-140, and 5754-1 and -3

90. Edgar Cayce 877-26

91. Luke 17:21

92. *Jiudan jing* ("Book of the Nine Elixirs") contains the earliest teachings about Taoist alchemy.

93. Edgar Cayce 2475-1

94. Edgar Cayce 900-331

95. Luke 11:34-36

96. Edgar Cayce 137-5 and 3744-2

97. Edgar Cayce 262-9

98. John 3:8

99. Edgar Cayce 256-1

100. Edgar Cayce 311-2

101. Edgar Cayce 281-13

102. Edgar Cayce 2539-2

103. Revelation 1:18 (when we interpret the spirit speaking to John with "a great voice like a trumpet" and identified as the "Alpha and Omega" as John's divine self awakened by being "in the spirit on the Lord's day" when the revelation occurred. Also, our ability to avoid the "second death" is found in Revelation 2:11 and 20:6.)

104. Edgar Cayce 281-37

105. Matthew 7:16-18

106. Edgar Cayce 262-20, 877-22, and 254-17

107. Edgar Cayce 1436-1, 2410-1, 3309-1, and 3605-1

108. ohn 3

109. There are several hundred passages in the Cayce files on "creative" and "creative forces." Here are two: 23-16: "Q: Any other advice at this time? A: Keep in the attitude of creative forces. Keep happy. Do not let anxiety of any nature disturb.» 78-4: «Q: Please give me any advice regarding the maintaining a more perfect mental and physical bal-

ance. A: In that as outlined may be that as an alignment of thought in a manner and direction as will give the proper attitude for the body, and the entity, in its activity. Not as a SERVILE attitude; NOT as one in a position of embarrassment; neither as one that would laud or applaud self for anything accomplished WITHIN self—either physically OR mentally; but rather in HUMBLENESS of heart, mind AND body TO be a channel for an ideal of WHATEVER making self may choose; were it only to THAT ideal of self's relationship to an individual, to self, or to the creative forces—for they are ONE, and each are a pattern of the other."

110. Matthew 25

111. John 17:5

112. Edgar Cayce 262-57, There are many more comments on infinity and timelessness in the Cayce files.

113. Revelation 1:10-12

114. See, *Edgar Cayce's Amazing Interpretation of the Revelation*, John Van Auken

115. John 10:10

116. Hanyu Pinyin, often abbreviated to pinyin, is the official romanization system for Standard Chinese in mainland China, adopted in 1958. It is often used to teach Standard Mandarin Chinese, which is normally written using Chinese characters. The Wade–Giles romanization system for Mandarin Chinese is the product of two British scholars: Sir Thomas Wade (August 25, 1818–July 31, 1895) and Herbert Allen Giles (December 8, 1845–February 13, 1935). Giles served as a British consular official in various parts of China from 1867–92.

117. See a glossary at, https://www.learnreligions.com/glossary-of-common-taoist-daoist-terms-3182620

118. *Quiet Sitting: The Daoist Approach for a Healthy Mind and Body*

119. Luke 24:36-43: "Jesus himself stood in the midst of them, and said to them, 'Peace to you.' But they were terrified and frightened, and supposed they had seen a ghost. And he said to them, 'Why are you troubled? And why do doubts rise in your hearts? Behold my hands and my feet, that it is I myself. Handle me and see, for a ghost does not have flesh and bones as you see I have.' When he had said this, he showed them his hands and his feet. But while they still did not believe for joy, and wondered, he said to them, 'Have you any food here?' So

they gave Him a piece of a broiled fish and some honeycomb. And He took it and ate in their presence."

120. Edgar Cayce 877-26

121. "Commentary by C. G. Jung", pages 81-137 of the original Wilhelm-Baynes book.

122. A Chinese Buddhist sutra (*Avatamsaka*, "Flower Garland Sutra") from the Hua-yen school composed during the reign of Empress Wu, 690-705 CE. It contains influences from the Taoist concepts of *activity to inactivity*, and *being to nonbeing*. The main tenet in Hua-yen philosophy is referred to as the principle of "dynamic Suchness." Known in Sanskrit as *tathata*, meaning the *ultimate inexpressible nature of all things*. This awareness is intuitively experienced in deep meditation.

123. Mark 12:28-34

124. Edgar Cayce 281-47, my italics

125. See *Edgar Cayce's Amazing Interpretation of the Revelation*, Van Auken, 2015, amazon.com

126. Edgar Cayce 1173-8

127. Edgar Cayce 281-16

128. Edgar Cayce 281-16

129. *Egyptian Book of the Dead*, Budge, 1895, The Papyrus of Ani, *The Hymn to Ra*: "I have come to the City of God, the region that is eternally old, with my soul (*ba*), double [spirit] (*ka*) and spirit-soul (*akhu*), to be a dweller in this land. Its God is the Lord of Truth." Akh and akhu are often translated as, "star" and "star being." This portion of us is eternal.

130. Edgar Cayce 900-181

131. Edgar Cayce 136-62

132. Luke 17:21 KJV

133. Edgar Cayce 622-6

134. Edgar Cayce 1632-2

135. Edgar Cayce 2677-1

136. Edgar Cayce 5155-1

137. Edgar Cayce 69-4

138. Edgar Cayce 278-1: "Life itself is an essence or manifestation of the divine Intelligence, or Force, that we call God. When there is incoordination between the mental, the physical and the spiritual body (which are One, represented by the Trinity—the Father, the Son and the Holy Spirit, in the spiritual world), we have what we call dis-ease. This may

grow into real disease. Our medical science has classified these into different names, because they affect different portions of the body. Now, any healing that may possibly come must be a re–coordinating of that physical being to that triune of force manifesting in our bodies. So, all healing must come from God. Whether the intelligence that brings that consciousness is from a drug, a mechanical appliance, the foods we eat, or what not, it is in its essence one and the same source."

139. John 4:24

140. Edgar Cayce 262–10

141. Edgar Cayce 262–79

142. Edgar Cayce 1183–1

143. https://www.sciencedaily.com/releases/2016/10/161005132823.htm

144. Edgar Cayce 281–28

145. Van Auken, John; *Passage in Consciousness: A Guide for Expanding Our Minds and Raising the Life Forces in Our Bodies through Deep Meditation*, Living in the Light, 2016. Available on amazon.com in Kindle version and paperback.

146. Edgar Cayce 914–1 and many more, for this is an often–repeated teaching.

147. Edgar Cayce 5367–1

148. John 3:13

149. John 14:4

150. Edgar Cayce 900–181

151. Edgar Cayce 1747–5

152. Edgar Cayce 3352–1

153. Edgar Cayce 257–201

154. Edgar Cayce 774–3, includes the affirmation quote following.

155. 3:16

156. Acts 2:3–4

157. John 4:24 and Hebrews 12:29

158. Edgar Cayce 281–13

159. Edgar Cayce 900–227

Other Books by John Van Auken

- *Passage in Consciousness: A Guide to Expanding Our Minds and Raising the Life Forces in Our Bodies through Deep Meditation*
- *Reincarnation & Karma: Our Soul's Past-Life Influences*
- *From Karma to Grace: The Power of the Fruits of the Spirit*
- *Edgar Cayce on the Spiritual Forces Within Us*
- *Angels, Fairies, Dark Forces, and the Elements: With the Edgar Cayce Perspective on the Supernatural World*
- *Edgar Cayce on Health, Healing, and Rejuvenation*
- *Edgar Cayce on the Mysterious Essenes: Lessons from Our Sacred Past*
- *2038: Great Pyramid Timeline Prophecy*
- *Edgar Cayce's Amazing Interpretation of The Revelation*
- *Hidden Teachings of Jesus*
- *A Broader View of Jesus Christ*
- *Edgar Cayce and the Kabbalah: A Resource for Soulful Living*
- *Ancient Egyptian Visions of Our Soul Life*
- *Mayan Toltec Aztec Visions of Our Soul Life*
- *Prophecies Converging in Our Times*

Index

A

Asclepius 12

B

backward-flowing 3, 45, 47
Baynes xxiii, xxiv, xxv, xxvi, xxxiv, xl, 1, 8, 21, 46, 78, 97, 104, 107, 108, 109, 119, 175, 176, 183
blood 31, 34, 54, 84, 113, 115, 173, 181
Bodhidharma 6
body vi, xi, xvi, xxiii, xxxi, xxxii, 1, 2, 4, 5, 6, 7, 8, 9, 10, 12, 13, 16, 23, 24, 25, 26, 29, 30, 31, 34, 36, 43, 44, 45, 48, 53, 54, 56, 57, 58, 67, 69, 70, 72, 74, 78, 80, 83, 84, 85, 87, 88, 89, 97, 100, 102, 108, 111, 114, 115, 116, 117, 118, 119, 120, 121, 122, 124, 129, 130, 131, 133, 134, 135, 136, 139, 140, 146, 150, 151, 152, 153, 154, 155, 156, 159, 160, 161, 162, 164, 165, 166, 170, 171, 172, 173, 177, 182, 183
brain 6, 9, 10, 23, 53, 67, 129, 130, 131, 153, 160, 161
Breath-energy 64, 69
breathing xi, 4, 9, 13, 54, 63, 64, 65, 66, 67, 71, 73, 79, 98, 122, 129, 131, 146, 150, 181
Buddha x, 11, 55, 68, 70, 86, 87, 103, 118, 123, 125, 134, 135, 136
Buddhism 56, 58, 171

C

cave 99, 100, 129
chakra 5, 6, 7, 9, 22, 24, 116, 130, 134, 154, 160, 161
chakras 4, 6, 9, 12, 24, 44, 102, 117, 125, 130, 146, 154, 160, 161, 171
chñi , 2
Christianity x, xix, xxvii, xxviii, xxxii, 21, 163
circulation 3, 4, 30, 43, 44, 45, 60, 61, 64, 72, 91, 92, 96, 97, 100, 117, 123, 125, 129, 130, 146
Cleary xxiv, xxv, xxvi, 3, 8, 13, 26, 35, 46, 66, 71, 77, 80, 85, 86, 92, 96, 104, 175, 176, 177, 179
consciousness xxi, xxvi, xxvii, xxx, 1, 5, 7, 9, 13, 19, 20, 21, 25, 27, 29, 30, 32, 34, 35, 36, 37, 39, 40, 41, 43, 45, 54, 56, 59, 60, 65, 66, 67, 72, 75, 86, 87, 88, 89, 98, 99, 101, 103, 107, 109, 113, 114, 115, 120, 121, 122, 124, 127, 131, 136, 140, 141, 144, 146, 152, 157, 159, 160, 161, 162, 164, 165, 166, 171, 173, 177, 178, 184
contemplation 47, 48, 55, 58, 59, 60, 103, 149
Creative Forces xxvii, 9, 11, 21, 25, 36, 41, 50, 140, 146, 153, 164, 166
Crucify 30, 69

E

Egypt xi, xviii, 6, 22, 26, 119, 125, 144, 164, 167, 176
Èlan vital , 2, 19
Elixir 13, 29, 30, 68, 96, 103
elixir 13
energy xi, xix, xxvi, xxxii, 2, 3, 5, 6, 9, 13, 19, 20, 22, 24, 25, 26, 29, 30, 34, 44, 45, 46, 47, 49, 50, 64, 65, 67, 68, 69, 73, 78, 80, 84, 88, 95, 98, 100, 102, 119, 122, 123, 129, 130, 131, 133, 134, 135, 154, 171
essence xvii, xviii, xx, xxi, xxii, xxvii, xxxii, xxxvii, 1, 2, 3, 5, 9, 19, 20, 21, 25, 56, 60, 67, 70, 100, 108, 109, 111, 112, 113, 116, 118, 119, 120, 122, 130, 136, 137, 140, 143, 144, 149, 150, 153, 164, 165, 173, 177, 183

F

Female 27, 178
female 27
Fixation 60
fontanelle 5, 9, 134, 153
four stages 10, 13
frontal lobe 9, 153, 160, 161

G

germinal vesicle 113, 114, 115, 116, 119, 120
glands 6, 7, 12, 31, 116, 117, 153, 154, 170, 172

A.R.E. PRESS

Edgar Cayce (1877–1945) founded the non-profit Association for Research and Enlightenment (A.R.E.) in 1931, to explore spirituality, holistic health, intuition, dream interpretation, psychic development, reincarnation, and ancient mysteries—all subjects that frequently came up in the more than 14,000 documented psychic readings given by Cayce.

Edgar Cayce's A.R.E. provides individuals from all walks of life and a variety of religious backgrounds with tools for personal transformation and healing at all levels—body, mind, and spirit.

A.R.E. Press has been publishing since 1931 as well, with the mission of furthering the work of A.R.E. by publishing books, DVDs, and CDs to support the organization's goal of helping people to change their lives for the better physically, mentally, and spiritually.

In 2009, A.R.E. Press launched its second imprint, 4th Dimension Press. While A.R.E. Press features topics directly related to the work of Edgar Cayce and often includes excerpts from the Cayce readings, 4th Dimension Press allows us to take our publishing efforts further with like-minded and expansive explorations into the mysteries and spirituality of our existence without direct reference to Cayce-specific content.

A.R.E. Press/4th Dimension Press
215 67th Street
Virginia Beach, VA 23451

Learn more at EdgarCayce.org. Visit ARECatalog.com to browse and purchase additional titles.

ARE PRESS.COM

Who Was Edgar Cayce?
Twentieth Century Psychic and Medical Clairvoyant

Edgar Cayce (pronounced Kay-Cee, 1877-1945) has been called the "sleeping prophet," the "father of holistic medicine," and the most-documented psychic of the 20th century. For more than 40 years of his adult life, Cayce gave psychic "readings" to thousands of seekers while in an unconscious state, diagnosing illnesses and revealing lives lived in the past and prophecies yet to come. But who, exactly, was Edgar Cayce?

Cayce was born on a farm in Hopkinsville, Kentucky, in 1877, and his psychic abilities began to appear as early as his childhood. He was able to see and talk to his late grandfather's spirit, and often played with "imaginary friends" whom he said were spirits on the other side. He also displayed an uncanny ability to memorize the pages of a book simply by sleeping on it. These gifts labeled the young Cayce as strange, but all Cayce really wanted was to help others, especially children.

Later in life, Cayce would find that he had the ability to put himself into a sleep-like state by lying down on a couch, closing his eyes, and folding his hands over his stomach. In this state of relaxation and meditation, he was able to place his mind in contact with all time and space—the universal consciousness, also known as the super-conscious mind. From there, he could respond to questions as broad as, "What are the secrets of the universe?" and "What is my purpose in life?" to as specific as, "What can I do to help my arthritis?" and "How were the pyramids of Egypt built?" His responses to these questions came to be called "readings," and their insights offer practical help and advice to individuals even today.

The majority of Edgar Cayce's readings deal with holistic health and the treatment of illness. Yet, although best known for this material, the sleeping Cayce did not seem to be limited to concerns about the physical body. In fact, in their entirety, the readings discuss an astonishing 10,000 different topics. This vast array of subject matter can be narrowed down into a smaller group of topics that, when compiled together, deal with the following five categories: (1) Health-Related Information; (2) Philosophy and Reincarnation; (3) Dreams and Dream Interpretation; (4) ESP and Psychic Phenomena; and (5) Spiritual Growth, Meditation, and Prayer.

Learn more at EdgarCayce.org.

What Is A.R.E.?

Edgar Cayce founded the non-profit Association for Research and Enlightenment (A.R.E.) in 1931, to explore spirituality, holistic health, intuition, dream interpretation, psychic development, reincarnation, and ancient mysteries—all subjects that frequently came up in the more than 14,000 documented psychic readings given by Cayce.

The Mission of the A.R.E. is to help people transform their lives for the better, through research, education, and application of core concepts found in the Edgar Cayce readings and kindred materials that seek to manifest the love of God and all people and promote the purposefulness of life, the oneness of God, the spiritual nature of humankind, and the connection of body, mind, and spirit.

With an international headquarters in Virginia Beach, Va., a regional headquarters in Houston, regional representatives throughout the U.S., Edgar Cayce Centers in more than thirty countries, and individual members in more than seventy countries, the A.R.E. community is a global network of individuals.

A.R.E. conferences, international tours, camps for children and adults, regional activities, and study groups allow like-minded people to gather for educational and fellowship opportunities worldwide.

A.R.E. offers membership benefits and services that include a quarterly body-mind-spirit member magazine, *Venture Inward*, a member newsletter covering the major topics of the readings, and access to the entire set of readings in an exclusive online database.

Learn more at EdgarCayce.org.

EDGARCAYCE.ORG